Practical Pattern Making

Practical Pattern Making

A Step-by-Step Guide

Lucia Mors De Castro & Isabel Sánchez Hernández

FIREFLY BOOKS

A Firefly Book

Published by Firefly Books Ltd. 2015

2nd printing, 2021

Publisher Cataloging-in-Publication Data (U.S.)

Mors, Lucia.
      Practical pattern making / Lucia Mors ; Isabel Sanchez.
[240] pages : photographs (some color) ; cm.
Includes index.
Summary: "This practical handbook explains everything on patternmaking in fashion. Through step-by-step exercises the reader will learn from the basic principles of the design to the patterns practical applications. This volume also presents interesting chapters on how to draw patterns, modeling and universal measurements." – from Publisher.
ISBN-13: 978-1-77085-611-0
1. Dressmaking – Pattern design. 2. Dressmaking — Patterns. I. Sanchez, Isabel. II. Title.
646.4072 dc23 TT520.M568 2015

Library and Archives Canada Cataloguing in Publication

Mors, Lucia, 1973-, author
      Practical pattern making / Lucia Mors, Isabel Sanchez.
Includes index.
ISBN 978-1-77085-611-0 (bound)   1. Dressmaking—Pattern design. 2. Dressmaking—Patterns. 3. Tailoring—Pattern design. 4. Tailoring—Patterns. I. Title.
TT520.M67 2015   646.4'072   C2015-900830-1

Published in the United States by
Firefly Books (U.S.) Inc.
P.O. Box 1338, Ellicott Station
Buffalo, New York 14205

Published in Canada by
Firefly Books Ltd.
50 Staples Avenue, Unit 1
Richmond Hill, Ontario L4B 0A7

Cover design: Erin R. Holmes / Soplari Design
Translation: Rita Granda

Printed in China

Conceived, and designed by
LOFT Publications
Via Laietana, 32, 4th, of. 92
08003 Barcelona, Spain
Managing editor: Claudia Martinez Alonso
Assistant editor: Ana Marques
Art Director: Mireia Casanovas Soley

CUT TO CUT
A book on dressmaking

The first documents on dressmaking date to the 16th century. They were plans for cutting that wasted the least possible amounts of cloth. At that time the use of a pattern adapted to body measurements was frowned upon since a good tailor could transfer measurements directly to the fabric and design the shape perfectly on the client. Each order was done separately and if the same client placed a new order the process would start over from the beginning. That is how individual made-to-measure designs emerged.

By the 19th century women's magazines included patterns. The importance of decoration and fabric design decreased while shape and body adaptation were given greater importance.

With the invention of the sewing machine, increasing industrialization and the beginnings of large-scale production, the use of standardized dressmaking sizes became crucial. The sizes were created by taking measurements from large population groups. This made the unlimited reproduction of a successful design possible, which completely revolutionized the world of fashion. Because of this, clients can now choose from an extensive supply of styles, materials and colors. When we choose a specific design from the great variety of options that we are presented with, because we think it matches our taste best, there is a great possibility that we have been influenced, in large part, by current fashion. If we decide to sew our own clothes despite the huge supply, maybe the biggest reason is to feel as comfortable as possible. Plus, it allows us to express our ideas and thoughts as reality. Satisfaction with our own creativity and for "doing-it-ourselves" makes a garment's qualities even more valuable.

To create fashion all you need is paper, pencils, a ruler and a table. You also need ideas, curiosity, ambition, concentration and perseverance. In the following pages, we present all of the current techniques, formulas and tricks to produce a garment that adjusts to an individual body. Starting with basic patterns, we introduce the development of creative design to stimulate an understanding and sensitivity towards body measurements before revealing the logical geometric rules of flexible design. The detailed design variations that are shown here are rooted in basic patterns; they only show a small part of the varied and infinite creative possibilities. Nevertheless, they contain a large number of routine ideas on learning and details that can be applied to any design idea if they are developed.

By dealing with these basic concepts, the thought and work process hidden behind a finished item of clothing is quickly captured. Further, this book tries to convey the varied language of shapes in fashion as well as the fascination that developing and creating garments, working with paper and cloth, awakens in us.

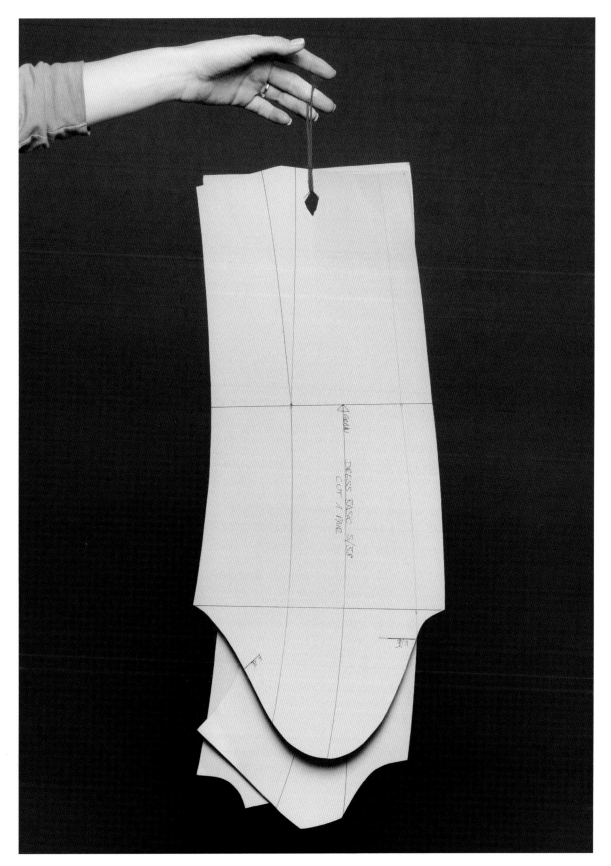

DEVELOPING PATTERNS

The term "pattern" describes a paper or cardboard plan that is used for cutting materials. Each part of an item of clothing, such as the front, the back, the pockets, the collar, the sleeves or the legs, needs its own pattern piece. This pattern can be created from an individual's measurements or from a standard size measured on an industrial scale.

Pattern-making is based on theory and calculations. It does not involve vague suggestions, but logical solutions embodied on paper. A pattern is a technical introduction that responds to a specific need and invites us to get down to work. It entails a complete design plan in simple paper form. A pattern guarantees the realization of a design whether as a single piece or in industrial production.

There are many pattern systems, and they all have advantages and disadvantages. The common characteristic is that they all use a specific order in formulas and modules that can be applied to obtain a reliable result when following the measurements taken. Therefore, it is important to understand the process from the beginning so that you have a solid base upon which to start developing and experimenting. The examples shown here do not belong to a complete pattern system but they are based on insights from the M. Müller & Sohn system, which can be expanded upon by sampling, experimenting and exchanging with friends and other pattern systems.

The challenge of pattern design is to create on a two-dimensional surface the basis for a three-dimensional garment. The pattern specifies both the surface size and the depth size. Often, the paper pattern takes on shapes that are difficult to understand with its curves and bumps. The plastic model is not revealed until the pattern is transferred to cloth, the individual pieces are sewn and the darts are added.

1-2-3-4. Darts are wedge-shaped folds that end in a point and are used with non-stretch fabric. They have an established position in basic pattern making and any necessary corrections to the darts are best made during a fitting. Meanwhile, dart positions are often confusing in pattern making as they disappear between the seams. Darts are drawn on the paper pattern in such a way that it is hard to know what they are; they look like decoration.

If you want to move a dart, keep in mind that its original position adapts best to the shape of the body. Therefore, a dart should only undergo a parallel move the exact distance needed, as in the waist dart in the image. We recommend never moving a dart more than 3-4 cm.

5-6. Another way to modify the position of a dart is to relocate it. First, determine the new location of the dart and draw it on the paper in the new position. Close the original dart and the corresponding volume will move to the new dart. By modifying the length of the dart in the new position it will appear wider or narrower but its effect on the pattern will not change.

7-8. A closed dart can be eliminated altogether. Nevertheless, as with a transfer, the dart's volume will not be lost but will "move" in another direction. Unlike modifying by moving the dart, the volume is not sewn but its width is used to obtain a larger diameter or a wider hem.

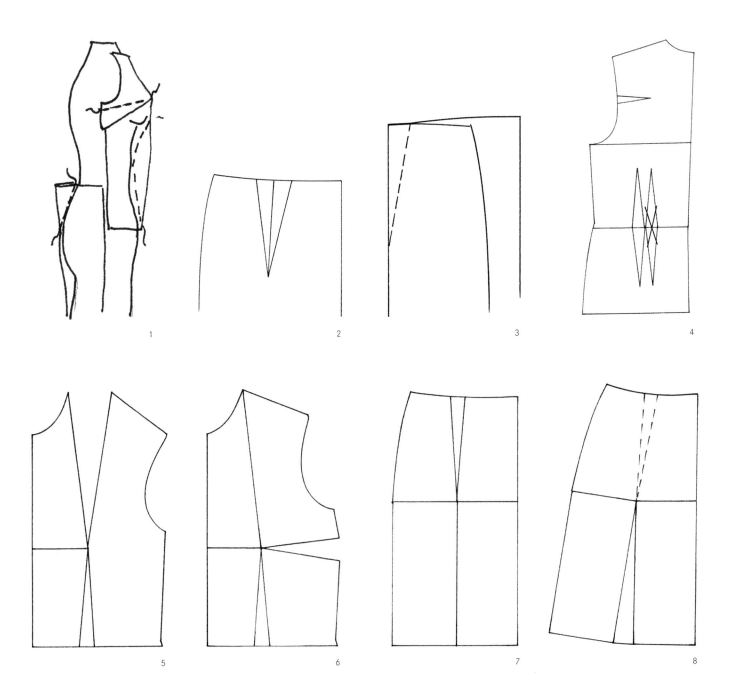

1   2   3   4

5   6   7   8

CREATIVE PATTERN MAKING

At the forefront of creative pattern-making is the idea of obtaining a perfect fit or silhouette, a solution with very specific details, a sense of fabric or color, or maybe it is just the satisfaction of wearing a unique garment.

When we imagine a design, it is recommended to start with a sketch before beginning to draw the pattern. That way, the details and the proportions will be clear. Design inspiration often comes from existing images such as fashion photographs or sketches, or from everyday images that are completely coincidental.

To reproduce a drawing or a photograph, it is very helpful to start with a precise analysis. Where exactly do the chest, the waist and the hip lines end? How do we adjust proportions, which are often stylized, to an actual pattern size? First, it is important to establish the relationship between the sizes of seams, flat areas and curves before putting them on paper. As a guide, photographs show the length, elbow or cuffs, if they are visible.

The pattern for an item of clothing always begins with a basic pattern. If it is correct, the modeling lines are drawn. These lines give the design its special shape and establish the position of the stitching, pockets, darts, etc. When drawing the modeling lines and establishing proportions, always keep in mind that we are working on a two-dimensional surface in order to obtain a three-dimensional product. For example, in a frontal image the area located between the side seam and the so-called vertical line of vision, or the furthest visible points, is usually outside of our field of vision. In a skirt this can often be 4 cm from the side seam.

Determining the lines of the design is not an easy task for those without any experience. Taking measurements of our body, or chest, will inspire confidence and help our eyes to get used to it. The relationship between the sizes of specialty mannequins, fashion sketches or photographs, and the pattern can be calculated with the help of some basic figures. First, we measure the distance from the waist to the neck on the basic pattern: for example, 37 cm. Then the same distance on the design: for example, 12 cm. If you divide 37 by 12, you get 3. In other words 1 cm of the sample corresponds to 3 cm of the pattern. This calculation also serves for length relationships. The silhouette and the width are valued for their proportions. Great accuracy and an inclination towards the middle ground is needed here given that, when we draw patterns, we usually move subtly between correcting the construction and the actual shape, logical deductions and a sense of lines and proportions.

Good pattern makers know how important it is to work as accurately as possible but they also know that their patterns have to adjust to a three-dimensional body through flexible fabric. The body does not have corners or completely straight lines. Therefore, we can only approach reality with patterns, and this shortfall is balanced by directly adjusting the garment to the body.

The same happens with the "implied laws" of tailoring. For example, our eyes and movements are used to female garments closing from right to left, and side zippers and asymmetrical decorations always being on the left side of the body. We need to know these conventions so that we can work around them when need be.

MODELING

Modeling is an ongoing form of creative development in patterns. Here, we work directly with the fabric on the tailor's mannequin to develop a shape or a complete garment. This results in a unique piece that the pattern can later be made from by transferring tracings and marks to the paper.

Modeling is a direct physical search for shapes, and this method of practical testing and discarding usually gives rise to completely new designs and ideas. For many, this process is simpler than the detour of drawing the patterns since the result of each action is directly visible. On the other hand, for others it seems too complicated to directly face a piece of cloth, shape it and transfer it to a pattern without any guide lines.

Certainly, modeling requires practice. Everyone should think about how to begin the process, where to place the pins, how to develop the shape without the material constantly moving from its position, how to cut and place the pieces, how to join them in a way that the resulting paper pattern will match the modeled piece exactly, and how to ensure that the final sewn model matches the actual design.

Despite this apparent complexity, modeling is critical for understanding pattern making and at least a few practical exercises should be attempted. For modeling, it is recommended to select a sample fabric with a weight similar to the desired garment. Also, it helps to mark on the mannequin the main measurements for the neck, chest, waist and hip sizes, and the main chest and sleeve insertion points with basting in different colors. Transfer these to the model before taking it off of the mannequin. Using these reference points you can transfer the new model lines to a basic pattern. Modeling and draping experiment with the complex relationships that exist between the body, the fabric and the shape, and let us see that the mystery of design is nothing more than a play between basic geometric shapes like straight lines, circles, curves, right angles and triangles. For example, if we try to draw the basic pattern starting with a fabric with straight angles on a tailor's mannequin, we quickly realize that darts are needed in some areas in order to give the fabric a shape, so that the cloth folds and the hem drops.

9-10. We find the triangle again in the outline of V-necklines or in the wedges created in a pleated skirt.

The triangle shape is used to get more volume by "reversing" pattern pieces, which is cutting and rotating them in opposite directions. The triangular wedges that are also included in the edges are useful in many situations.

11-12-13-14-15. Linking and rotations are more advanced modeling exercises that require soft fabrics with a little give. Two pieces with their corresponding shapes are rotated between each other and, as a result, the excess fabric creates folds.

16-17. A circle with an opening and a spiral are set apart because the outside diameter is always greater than the inner diameter. This is how we get the fall of a skirt, for example. A spiral creates ripples that can be used for many things such as frills, which are droopy bell-shaped decorations.

18-19. When placing the fabric on the mannequin, make sure the direction of the fabric grain remains vertical and moves parallel to the center front and center back. That way, the cross grain should always remain horizontal on the chest and the shoulder blades. For example, if we want to transfer the grain direction to a role of fabric, we must look at the selvage or pull on a thread of the fabric. If the darts are hidden, the fabric should envelope the mannequin without wrinkling or stretching.

Direct work on the tailor dummy or on the model is essential for establishing the volume and silhouette as well as the neck, pockets and sleeves. It is also helps to determine if the shape fits.

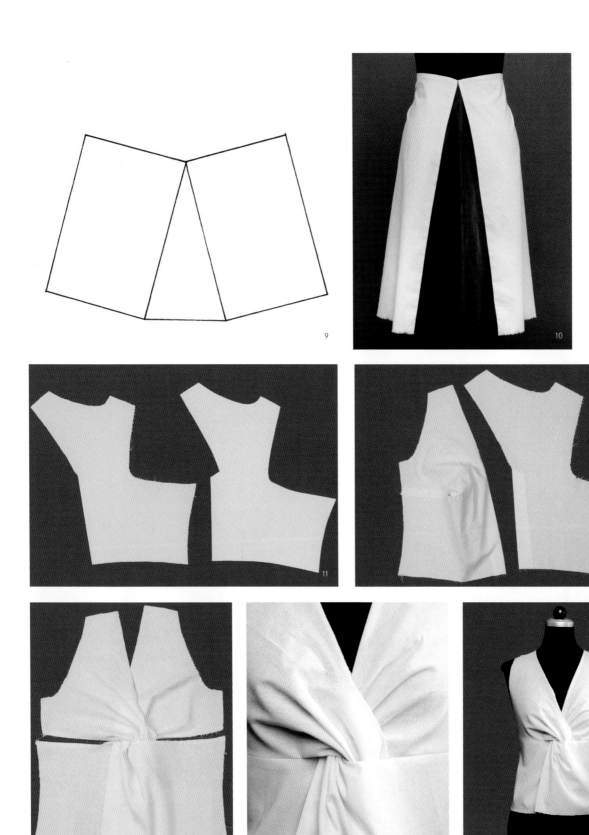

9

10

11

12

13

14

15

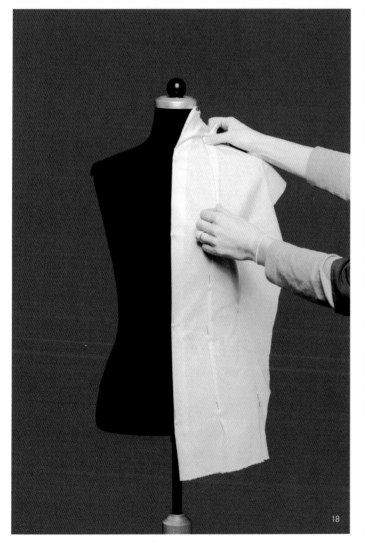

DRAWING PATTERNS

For practical reasons, we recommend beginning by following the instructions with exact measurements then later developing creations on the basic pattern. When basic patterns are perfect, as in the cloth prototypes that are already tested and modified, they establish the best preparatory requirements for experimenting without limits with pattern-making. There is always the strong likelihood that this pattern will also be adjusted.

Finally, we can venture into working with model patterns. Since the human body usually is symmetrical, in basic patterns and in most model patterns only one half is drawn. In other words, we work with half of the size measurements, which are adequate from the center front to the center back. Before cutting the cloth, it should be folded in half so that the center front or the center back of the pattern piece remains exactly on the cloth fold line. In an industrial environment and with asymmetrical patterns, the cut is not doubled and patterns are drawn in full. The right angle between the center front and the center back, as well as all of the joining areas, is extremely important so that when the cloth is opened or pieces are joined there are no issues or holes. Therefore, during pattern-making all of the pieces should be joined by the seams and compared.

When the pattern pieces are ready, ordered labeling is crucial. Numbering helps to see the whole at a glance and prevents the loss of small pieces. Marking the direction of the grain guarantees that each pattern piece will be cut with the correct alignment.

Instructions minimize possible mistakes and speed up the cutting process considerably. They indicate how many times a piece is cut, whether the same piece is cut twice or once with the fabric folded, or if it should be reinforced with an interfacing.

Accurately marking pieces and joining points will help with deciphering the pattern later. This is done with crosses in the edges of the pattern to mark chest, waist and hip lines, sleeve insertion marks, dart positions and the width of any sewn additions. Letters and special marks are also used when drawing patterns but they will become familiar with time. The following lists a small selection of standard marks:

AM % 0-3 cm	↓	∟	X	X···O	CF Fold
Unlike usual practice, in pattern making the symbols % and – mean "minus" and "up to" respectively.	The arrow marks the direction of the grain.	This symbol indicates a right angle.	A cross on a dart means it will be omitted.	In pleats, an arrow indicates the direction of the pleat. To further clarify, the symbol X joined to O can also be used. Shaded areas are omitted or altered.	CF and CB mean center front and center back respectively. "Cut on the center line" or "double" means that the piece should be cut on folded cloth.

TAKING MEASUREMENTS

To create patterns that are adjusted to the measurements and characteristics of a specific body, we must measure that body carefully. A made-to-measure pattern that is tested then fixed will adjust perfectly to the needs of an individual body, highlighting the most attractive parts while hiding defects.

Two people are needed for taking measurements since the one being measured should be standing upright in a natural posture. Measurements can be taken while wearing underwear or a light dress but not in a sweater and blue jeans since these will greatly influence the measuring results. In cases where the measuring requirements are very precise, such as the corset of a wedding dress, it is recommended to always wear the same bra from the first measuring to the last fitting.

Before taking measurements and creating the pattern, the body should be observed and drawn with precision from various perspectives. Focus especially on how the contours of the body are distributed, what curves are shown and what deviations from the norm can be assessed already from working with the pattern. All of the measurements should be taken with the tape close to the body, not too tight and not too loose.

20-21. It works best to start with a measuring tape, specifically one with small clasps at the ends so that it can be closed. Wrap the tape around the waist and secure it with the clasps at a suitable point. When measuring, the waist size (WS) should always be taken at the narrowest part of the trunk.

22-23-24. The next thing to measure is the chest size (CS). For this, the measuring tape is placed in front of the highest part of the chest then circles the body by going under the arms and rising up a bit in the area of the shoulder blades.

25. The hip size (HS) is the horizontal circumference of the body measured at the widest part of the backside. It works best to take this measurement from the side.

26. The distance between the circumference of the hip and the waistline is the hip height (HH), which is usually 19–22 cm below the waist.

27-28. Next, measure the shoulder width (SW), the sleeve length (SL) and the position of the elbow. The shoulder width is obtained by measuring from the base of the neck to the shoulder bone. For the elbow position, measure from the shoulder bone to the point on the outside of the elbow. For the sleeve length, measure from the shoulder bone to the wrist.

The measurements of the arm and forearm contours should also be taken in cases where the arms are very thick or very thin.

29. The measurement of the back arc (BA) determines the position and depth of the sleeve hole. In order to obtain this figure, begin by placing a strip of paper under the arm that reaches to the spinal column. Measure from the upper cervical vertebrae to the very top of the horizontal strip of paper for the back arc measurement.

30. Back length (BL) is also measured from the upper cervical vertebrae but this time to the extreme inside of the waistline. The back length together with the front length is one of the most important measurements in pattern-making. This figure should be measured with great precision and compared to the measurement chart. If there are great deviations between the measured figure and the measurement chart, it is best for a beginner to use the numbers on the chart.

31. Back width (BW) is measured approximately at chest height, in the inner part of the shoulder blade. It should be measured flat from one sleeve hole to the other with the arms relaxed and hanging down. Mark two broad lines here to pinpoint where the back and arms join.

32. For the next step, place the measuring tape in front at the base of the neck. The chest depth (CD) is measured from here to the tip of the chest while the front length (FL) is measured to the inside of the waistline.

Compare the measurements taken to the measurement chart and match them to a dressmaking size. Use chest size (CS) as your guide and choose the dressmaking size that is the most similar to your chest size. It could be that the other measuring results do not match those on the list or that some measurements are missing. Why? The main measurements of height (H), chest size (CS), waist size (WS), hip size (HS) and sleeve length (SL), taken with the measuring tape held close to the body, appear right on the pattern. On the other hand, additional measurements such as back arc (BA), back length (BL), hip height (HH), chest depth (CD), front length (FL) and back width (BW) are measured and compared with the measurement chart. When in doubt, beginners should use the measurement in the chart in order to eliminate most measuring errors.

The collar (C), armhole diameter (AD) and chest width (CW) are always calculated given that they are difficult measurements and the risk of measuring incorrectly is quite high. We can calculate these measurements from a 31½ inch CF with the help of the following formulas:

C Collar
1/10 of 1/2 CD chest depth + 2 cm
AD Armhole diameter
1/8 CD chest depth %1.5 cm
CW chest width
1/4 CD chest depth % 4 cm

Once the relevant measurements have been calculated, we can continue making the pattern. Keep in mind that to give a certain freedom of movement to the garment it is important to detail extra measurements such as back arc (BA), back width (BW), armhole diameter (AD), chest size (CS), and chest depth (CF).

These extra measurements depend on the relevant model, the material used and individual preferences in dressing. Nevertheless, here are some guiding figures:

	Dress	Fitted jacket	Loose jacket	Short coat to long coat
	1 cm	1.5-2 cm	2-2.5 cm	3-3.5 cm
Back height BH	1 cm	1.5–2 cm	2– 2.5 cm	3–3.5 cm
Back width BW	0.5 cm	1 cm	1-1.5 cm	1.5–2 cm
Armhole diameter AD	1.5 cm	2 cm	2.5–3 cm	3–4 cm
Chest width CW	1.5 cm	1.5–2 cm	2 cm	2–2.5 cm
1/2 Chest size CS	3.5 cm	4.5–5 cm	5.5–6.5 cm	6.5–8.5 cm

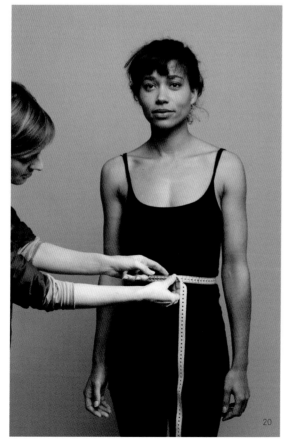

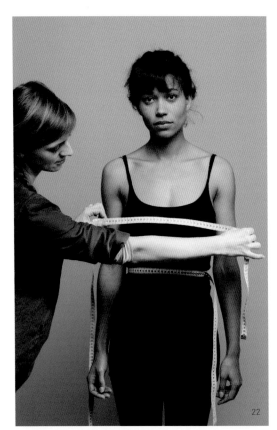

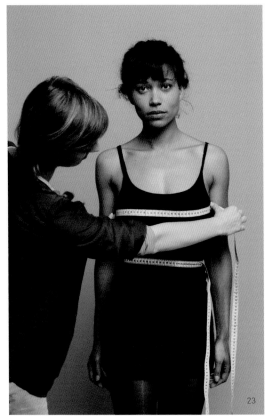

26

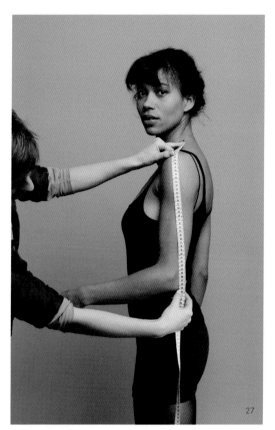

27

28

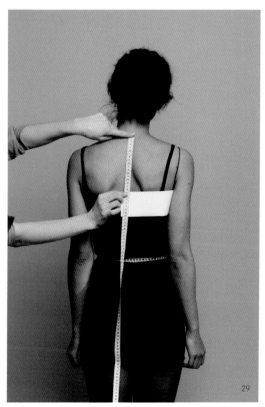

29

THE MEASUREMENT CHART

Measurement chart (see page 238) can be used as templates. They are useful for organizing all of the measurements you will need to create your first pattern. With the charts, you can proceed confidently knowing you will not forget any of the measurements and that everything is calculated correctly.

Along with the measurements, other basic information can be added to the chart, such as the client's name, the date and updated entries since the body naturally changes with time. It is best to make "observations on the figure" regularly from a specific distance. If you make accurate observations when the pattern is created, it will simplify the decisions that have to be made later. Draw the shapes of specific body types directly on the sketch of the basic pattern and on the figure accompanying the chart.

It is important to determine any deviations from the "normal body", even though a "normal body" does not really exist. Some of the main features to keep in mind are: stooped, tilted or very rigid postures, different shoulder heights, the thickness of the shoulder blades, the height and shape of the chest, the shape of the abdomen and hip, the curve of the spine, and the thickness of muscles, calf muscles and knees. Ensure your measurements are as accurate as possible by repeatedly checking and altering your pattern from start to finish. Measure twice cut once!

In the upper part of the measurement chart, record the basic measurements taken such as height (H), chest circumference

(CC), waist circumference (WC), hip circumference (HC) and individual hip depth (HD), which is the vertical distance from the waist to the hip, and the shoulder width (SW). Recording the halves, quarters and eighths of these measurements will speed up the process for creating the pattern design.

On pages 238 to 240 are the figures from the measurement chart and those that are calculated using formulas. When in doubt, it is best for beginners to use the calculated measurements. The information is entered then, based on "normal body" measurements, it is added and the final calculation is made.

Measure and note the sleeve length (SL), the upper arm measurement (UAM) and the sleeve edge width (SEW). Calculate the sleeve crown height (SCH) and the sleeve width (SlW) with the appropriate formulas.

Once the measurement chart is completely filled in, you can begin the real work on the basic patterns.

In the following pages we will explain step by step how to create basic patterns for skirts, dresses and fitted garments. This will serve as a basic methodology for creative pattern making that can be applied to any set of measurements. The following examples offer an overview of the endless possibilities for variation in pattern making. They also pass down to us basic techniques such as how to deal with darts and pleats and how to create a silhouette.

BASIC PATTERN FOR STRAIGHT SKIRT

Measured sample sizes:
(WC) Waist Circumference
68 cm – 34 cm
(HC) Hip Circumference
98 cm – 49 cm
(HD) Hip Depth 20 cm
(SL) Skirt Length 60 cm

Calculated sample sizes:
1/2 WC Waist Circumference
(34 cm) + 1 cm extra width =
    35 cm
1/2 HC Hip Circumference
(49 cm) + 1 cm extra width =
    50 cm
Intake (difference between HC
    and WC) = 15 cm
Distribution of the intake:
side seam: 7 cm;
front piece: 2.5 cm;
back piece: 5.5 cm.

The basic pattern for a straight skirt can be used as the starting point for most skirt patterns. To create one, always draw a straight line falling from the waist; this gives a perfect fit and any changes can be made easily with a calculated ratio. The skirt type adjusts to the body with the span of the basic pattern beginning at the widest part of the body: the hip circumference. Reduce this measurement to find the waist circumference, which is smaller. The difference between the two circumferences is called the intake. Depending on the shape of the body and the skirt pattern, the distribution of the intake varies from front to back and should be adjusted frequently during the fitting stage.

1-2: Start the basic pattern at the center front with point 1. To find point 2, draw a line 20 cm straight down; this is the hip depth.

1-3: To find point 3, draw a 60 cm line from point 1; this is the length of the skirt. It can be shortened or lengthened later. From points 1, 2 and 3 draw lines to the right at right angles.

1-5: To find point 5, from point 1 draw the waistline (half of the hip circumference plus 49 cm + 1 cm extra width).

5-7: To find the center back line, draw the 60 cm skirt length from point 5. The pattern will be placed on this line later when the fabric is cut.

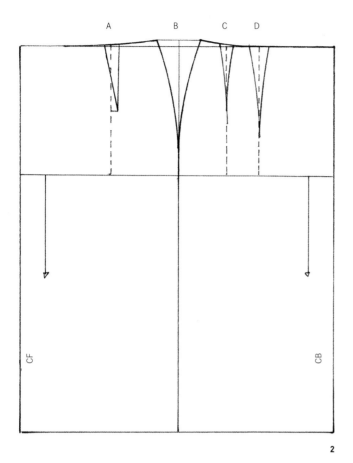

A   B C D

CF

CB

2

3

4-6: To calculate the baseline for the side seam, divide section 1–5 in two then use this measurement to draw a line from point 1 to point 4. To find point 6, measure that same distance from point 3 then join point 4 to point 6.

The left rectangle is the front of the skirt and the right is the back piece.

2. To fit the skirt to the shape of the body, calculate the intake at the waistline. Following the intake ratio, remove a total of 7 cm from the side seam, 2.5 cm from the front piece and 5.5 cm from the back piece. All that is needed in the back piece is a dart measuring at most 3–4 cm. If the intake is greater, distribute the total amount across two darts as in the following example. To draw the darts, follow these steps:

Dart A is located 6–8 cm from the side seam and incorporates 2.5 cm of the intake. It should be 9–11 cm long. Fold the end of the dart 1 cm to the right for a better fit.

Side seam B is 7 cm from the center with 3.5 cm on each side.

The arch of the side seam is marked according to the curve of the body and reconnects with the straight side seam at line 2, which is the maximum hip depth.

Dart D is located half way between the side seam and the cutting line; here, the intake is 3 cm in width and between 14 cm and 15 cm in length.

Dart C is located between the side seam and dart D. It is 2.5 cm wide and 12–13 cm long.

Add 1 cm to the side seam's base line to adjust for the curve of the body and remove another 0.5 cm from darts A and C. Draw the waistline in a circle; darts C and D on the back piece of the skirt should be slightly convex.

3. Draw the curve of the hip on the side seam with a French curve and, depending on the shape of the body, join the straight side seam at the maximum point on the hip line. Adjust this curve frequently during fittings.

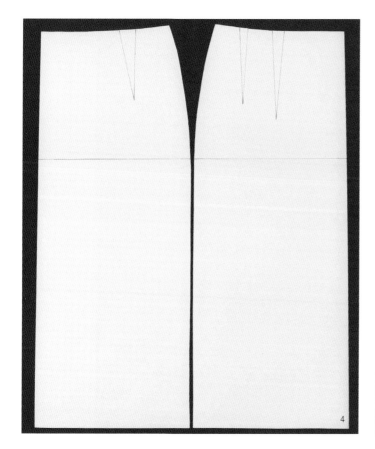

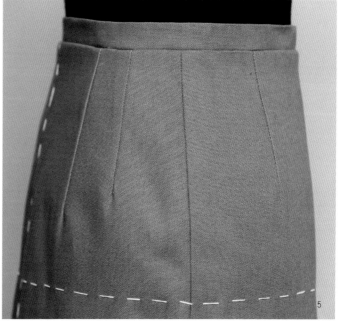

4. Copy the two halves of the skirt, the front and the back, and accurately draw the hip line and the darts. The number and shape of the darts will vary depending on the shape of the body. They have to be adjusted to individual characteristics often during fittings. For example, if a woman has a rounded belly, two darts might be needed in the front piece.

5. During the first fitting, make sure the side seams are always at the sides of the body. To finish, test the darts and reduce or add new darts as needed.

SIMPLE SKIRT
WITH OVERLAPPING FOLDS

1. Infinite variations can be created from the basic skirt pattern. The one shown here has two overlapping folds in the front piece and lightly hugs the silhouette. The appropriate fabric for this skirt would have a bit of body and an iridescent sheen. The entire width of the front piece is drawn here, because it is asymmetrical.

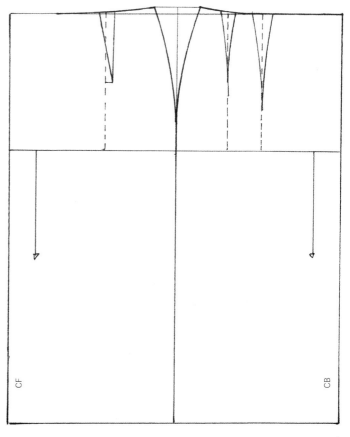

1

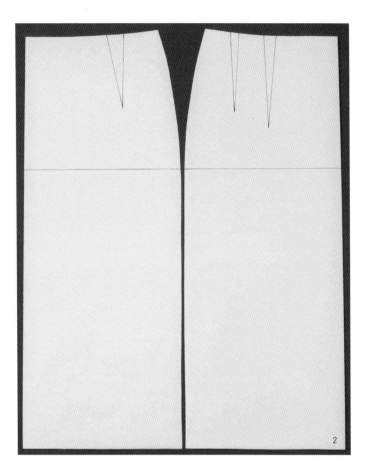

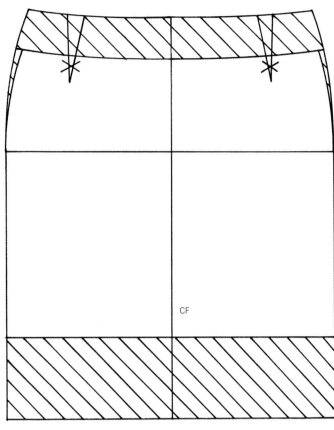

CF

2

3

2-3. Since the basic pattern reaches from the waist to the knee, shorten the hem by 12 cm for this skirt. Also, the waistband drops down by 6 cm. This sketch shows the doubled front piece with the center front in the middle. By lowering the waistband, the darts are reduced to small points of approximately 1 cm that are not sewn for aesthetic reasons. Instead trim the excess dart volume from the side seams. Follow the same steps for the back: lower the waistline and trim the width of the dart from the side seams.

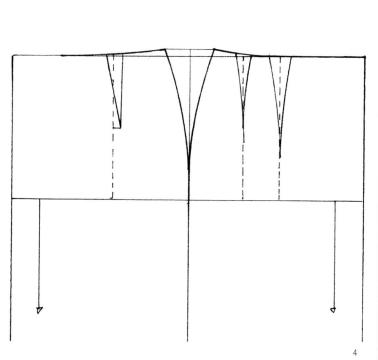

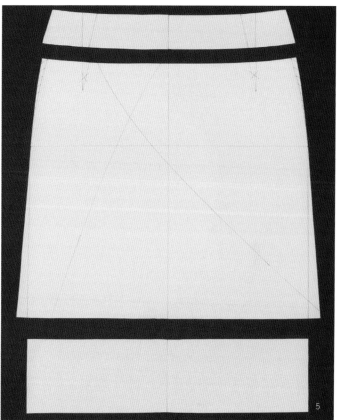

4-5. For a simple silhouette, widen the hem by 2 cm at the side seams so that the resulting seam will reach the hip depth of the original side seam. Make the same alteration to the back. In the front piece, establish the position of the folds and draw them with a slightly curved line. The position and shape of the folds depends on the individual design.

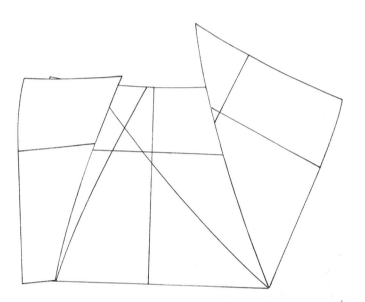

6

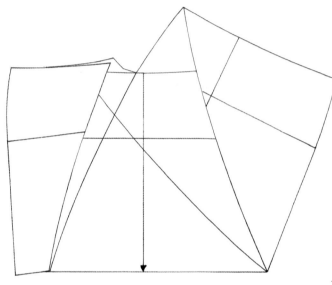

7

6. When overlapping the two folds it is important that the extent of the upper fold has the length needed to allow the inner fold to lie flat underneath. The front pattern piece shows the smooth skirt. The additional volume needed in the fabric to create the folds is now introduced in the pattern. For this, attach two side pieces that will extend from the side seam to the crossed fold lines that are marked. Trim the copied pieces but leave the original front piece intact. Place the additional trimmed pieces on the edge of the pattern piece so that the points touch at the hem. In the waist area, the distance of the position equals the width of the folds loosely tied. Now join the side pieces.

7. In the next step, fold the paper on the edge of a table, following the lines of the folds. Place the folds in the positions they will later have on the fabric. It is not easy to add the curvature of the fold lines since the paper is not as manageable as the fabric. Nevertheless, it is worth the extra effort since a slight curvature produces a more attractive folded effect and is more striking. Of course, the lines can also be straight, vertical or diagonal from the waist to the hem. If the waistline is evened off and cut straight, it will produce a serrated effect at the waist when the cut pieces are opened. This is actually due to the volume of the folds, and the amount of fabric that the folds need to expand.

8. It is helpful to mark the location and shape of the folds on the fabric with chalk or stitches so that the fabric can be shaped by hand then set with an iron.

TULIP SKIRT WITH ANGLED POCKETS AND ROUNDED WAISTBAND

1. In this variation of the straight cut skirt, we work with the so-called "cut edges" by cutting the pieces of paper and rotating the different pattern pieces. This creates additional volume that will later be adjusted to the body with seams or pleats.

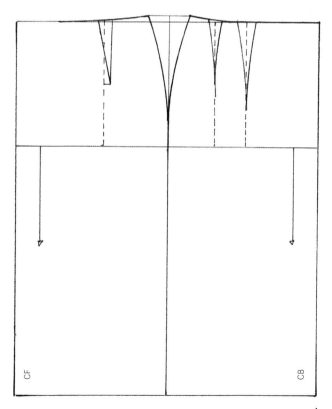

1

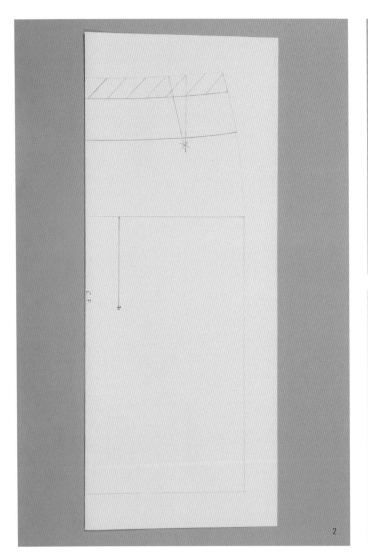

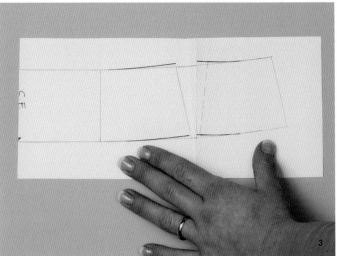

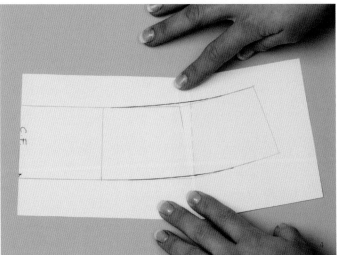

2. If you do not want to place the skirt right on the waist, it can be lowered by 4–6 cm from the basic pattern. To create the waistband in the shape of a belt, straighten the desired width of 6 cm at the new waistline.

3-4. Add the dart from the basic pattern to this paper pattern. This will allow us to eliminate the volume of the darts so that the waistband adjusts to the rounded waist, and we avoid having to sew unsightly darts. To do this, fold the paper along the dart line, creating a rounded waistband and even cutting edges. Remember to maintain right angles at all of the corners: the outside edge, the back, the front center and the sides.

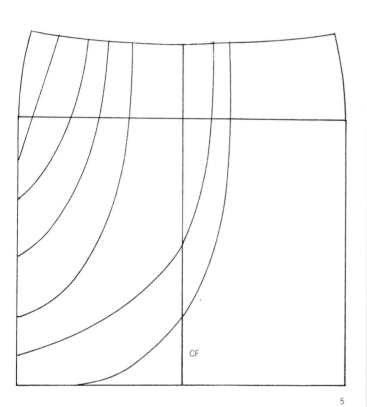

5

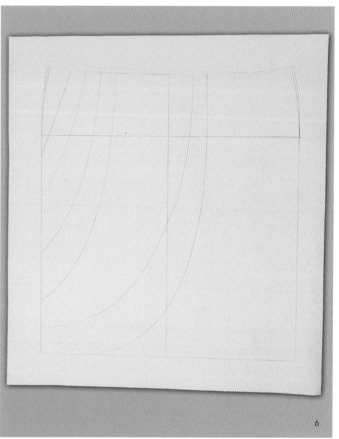

6

5-6. When the pleats and the rounded outline for the front hem have been marked, work on the entire pattern, as in the previous example with overlapping folds, not just the front half, as in the basic skirt pattern. Draw the positions, shapes and length of the pleats as per the desired design. This model has three side pleats and an angled pocket.

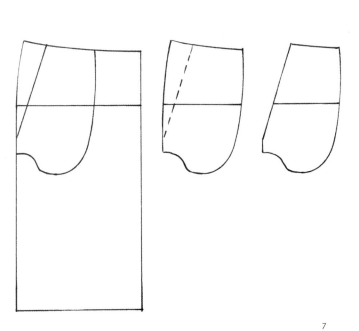

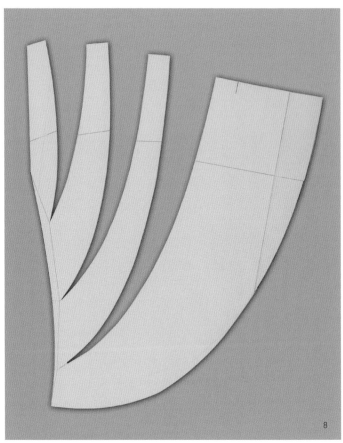

7. Mark the pocket on the side of the skirt; it should be as large as a dinner plate. The inside pocket reaches the side seam and replaces the piece of skirt eliminated by the angled opening. The outside pocket starts at the edge of the opening and can be cut from fabric liner. Close both parts of the pocket at the waistband and the side seam then sew the pocket pieces together.

8. Next, cut and fold the lines for the pleats. The pattern pieces remain joined at the side seam, which is where the pleats come in. For aesthetic reasons, there is no seam on the waistband. Instead, the front waistband circles around to join the back waistband and both pieces are sewn on to the skirt.

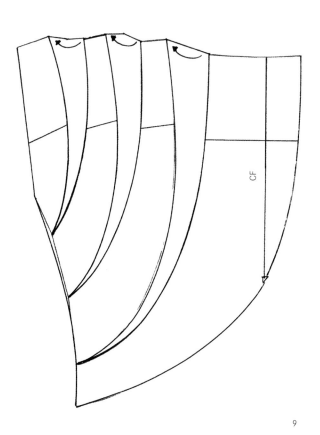

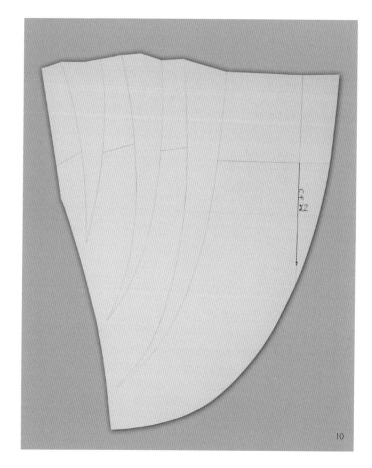

9-10. After trimming the pleat lines, you will have pattern pieces that move freely but hang together at the side seam. These pieces will move with the volume of the pleats, which is the amount for the desired extent of the pleat. All of these pattern pieces are held down with additional paper. We now have the front piece of the skirt. Next, even off the side seam by marking and trimming the corners. Fold the paper for the type and direction of pleat desired, and trim the cut edges so that the waistline is straight once the paper is folded. The unfolded paper will be serrated at the waistline and must be followed closely when the fabric is cut as this will give the volume needed for the pleats to look their best when they are folded.

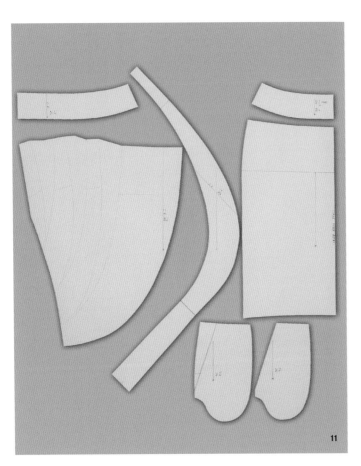

11. These are the finished pattern pieces: the front and back pieces, the front waistband, the joined front and back waistband, and the inside and outside pockets.

12. Make sure that all of the corners on the pattern pieces have right angles since this is the only way to avoid peaks and straight angles when the pieces of fabric are sewn together.

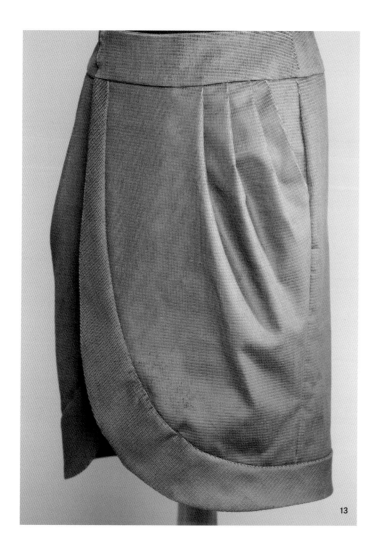

13. When the skirt is sewn, it is important to have enough intersecting lines and to join the waistbands together as usual, because the curves in the fabric expand easily.

JACKET WITH FRILLED COLLAR AND RAGLAN SLEEVES

1. The basic dress pattern on page 60 is used here since this type of jacket is relatively narrow at the shoulders and the waist. The width needed for the jacket is obtained by juxtaposing pieces. The special shape of the frilled collar is further enhanced with two different fabrics. In this example, a raglan sleeve is used to extend the basic pattern.

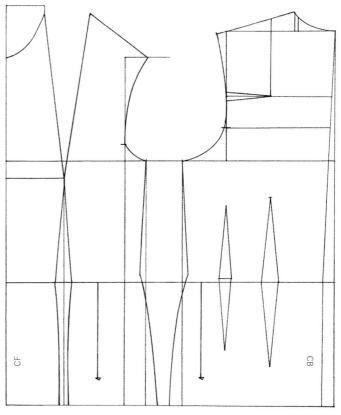

CF

CB

1

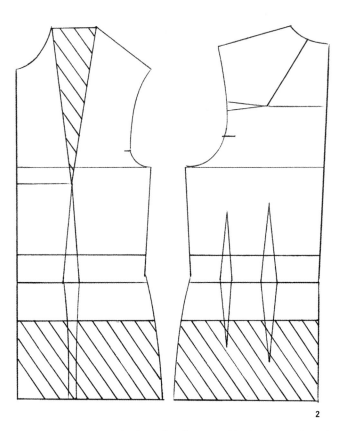

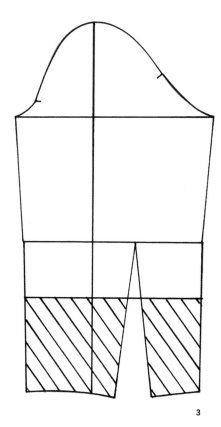

2. Begin by drawing the lines for the waist. In this case, place the lines 5 cm above the waist and 7 cm below. Omit the area that is left on the bottom half since this jacket is fitted at the waist. Prepare the layout of the darts on the upper part of the jacket. The front dart is positioned to expand the waist while the back dart is an aesthetic detail placed on the neck.

3. The raglan sleeve is made from the basic sleeve pattern on page 68. Draw a line from the highest point on the sleeve to the hem to produce the back dividing line. Now cut the sleeves to the desired length, in this case 42 cm.

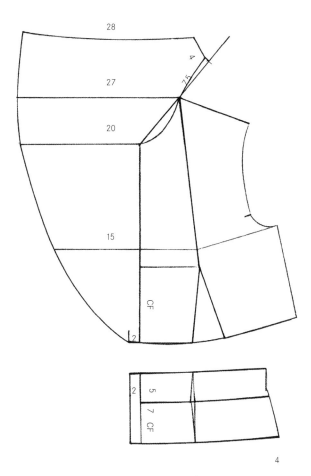

4

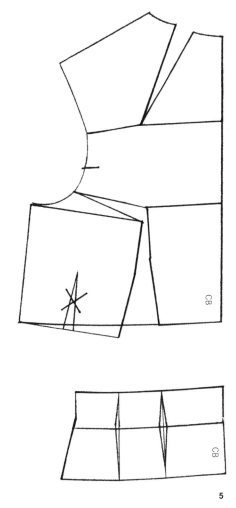

5

4. Next, separate the waistbands from the upper part of the jacket. The chest dart will be placed at the waist.

For the collar in the front, draw a line from the edge of the collar to the end of the neck hole. From there, draw a straight line matching the measurement of the back neck hole. Move up 1cm from that point and draw a slightly rounded line for the neck extension.

Determine the height and width of the collar. The measurements shown here are only recommendations since the collar can be designed with more or less volume. Nevertheless, make sure the collar tucks in at the joining point approximately 1.5–2 cm from the front center.

The upper part of the jacket has more volume because of the waist darts. This excess is arranged and adjusted across the entire waistband or it can be concentrated in one specific area.

Attach the waistband and include the darts in the pattern. The excess material from the center of the dart can be eliminated from the side seam after the fitting.

5. Cut and rotate the darts toward the armhole in the back for the width needed for the extension. The resulting gap will be joined when the extension is sewn to the waistband and the armhole will return to its original position. The size of the opening can be adjusted as desired or in relation to the front piece. To make the piece looser, do not sew the second dart.

The pieces on the hemline of the upper part are shifted across the opening. Trim the opening again and even it off.

As in the front piece, place the darts on the waistband. Place the upper and lower parts of the back on the center back fold.

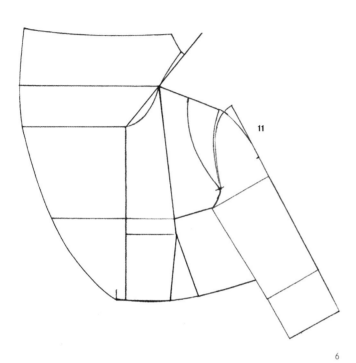

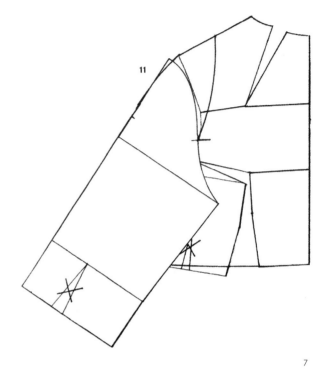

6. Before cutting the sleeve along the already drawn center line, extend a line 11 cm from the upper part of the sleeve. This reference point will be used later to even off the length of the shoulder seams.

Place the left sleeve piece on the front pattern piece so that the two sleeve drawings overlap. Add 1 cm at the end of the shoulder line for the extra length needed for the shoulder pad.

Since the sleeve covers part of the jacket and it is impossible to cut across it, draw a separation seam for the time being.

This separation seam can be a free-style curve from any point on the neck hole or the shoulder seam to the inserted sleeve pieces. For this model, separate both pattern pieces. The seam ends at the curved edges of the jacket sleeves and the sleeve.

7. For the back, repeat these steps with the right sleeve piece and overlap the drawings of both sleeves. Measure the shoulder seam for the back piece before stitching. Since the front shoulder seam is 11 cm long (see above) add an extra 0.6 cm to the matching back shoulder seam so that both pieces can be sewn together.

Ignore the hem dart in the pattern because this sleeve is straight. If the sleeve hem is too full, eliminate the extra volume from the side seam.

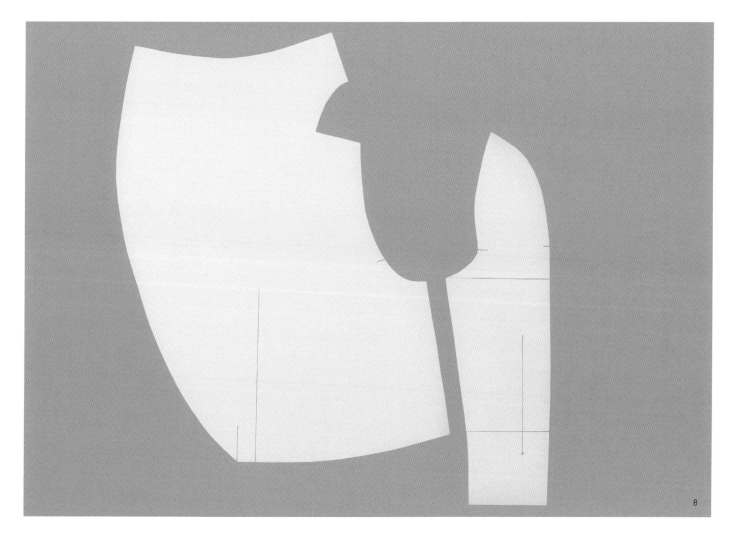

8. The photograph shows the drawing of the layout of the sleeves after separating along the new line. The shape of this line can be loosely drawn and it should cross the sleeve drawings. Both the front and back shoulder lines should be the same length.

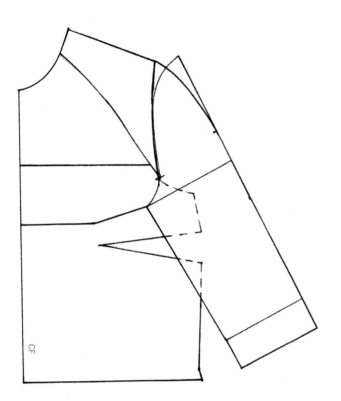

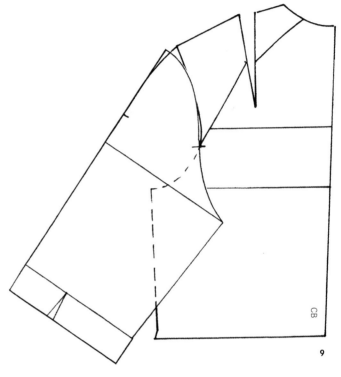

9

9. The main thing to keep in mind for the layout of the raglan sleeves is that the drawings of the sleeves and the torso must always overlap properly. The back piece always faces towards the front piece and the sleeve shoulder seams should be the same length. Also, leave between 1 and 1.5 cm at the shoulders for the shoulder pads.

By contrast, the separation line for the raglan can be loose. Its position depends on the desired design. It can go from the neck hole above the shoulder or from the front half above the point where the sleeve joins the side seam. Next, copy the pieces that overlap. The sketches that are shown here illustrate the separation of the raglan sleeve from the neck hole.

10. View of the finished pieces: the front and back sleeves, upper front and back jacket pieces, front and back waistbands. A small pocket can be added to the front waistband as an extra detail.

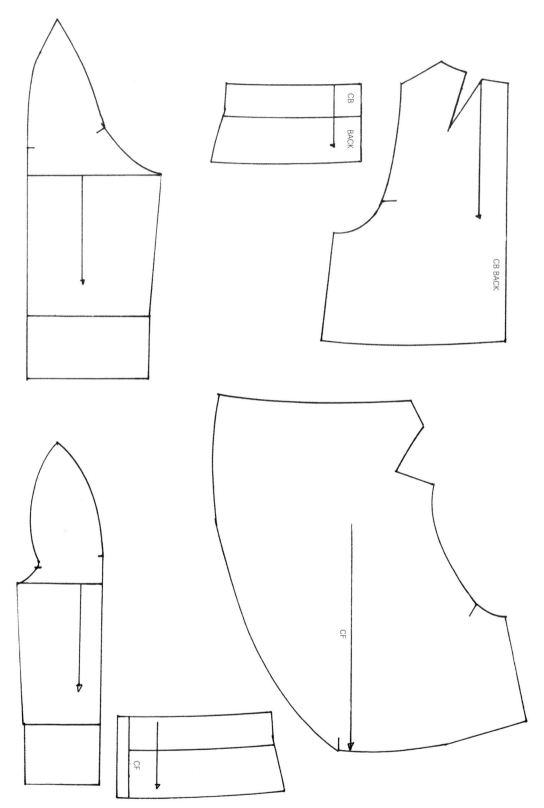

CB

BACK

CB BACK

CF

CF

10

11. The back view shows the raglan seam and the aesthetically placed oblique darts. Here, the dart does the job and is pleasing to the eye.

12. The frilled collar is especially attractive because of the contrasting colors used. The folds can be left to hang freely or they can be attached with a fastener.

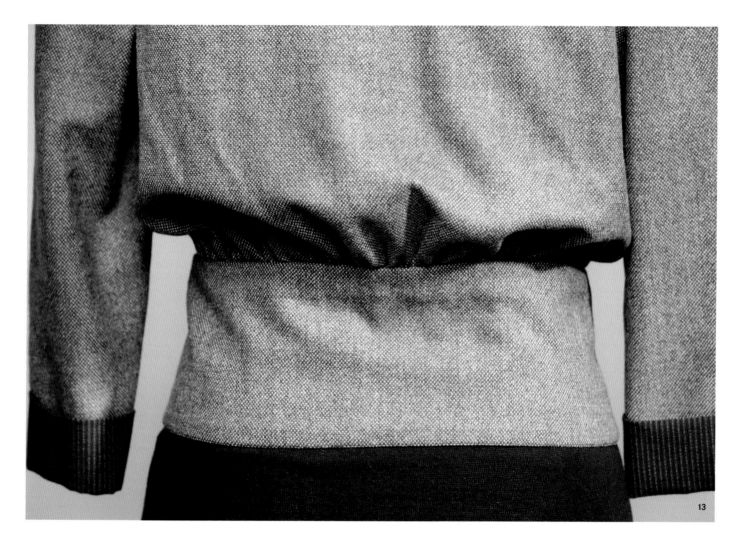

13

13. The fullness of the upper part of the jacket is adjusted and held at the waist. This produces a voluminous effect in contrast to the waistband that hugs the waistline.

FITTED JACKET WITH SHOULDER DETAIL

1. This jacket shows how to customize a double-seamed sleeve with an interesting detail on the shoulder.

The change in this cut is best suited to those who are advanced but, as the pattern shows, there is relatively little effort required compared to the effect achieved.

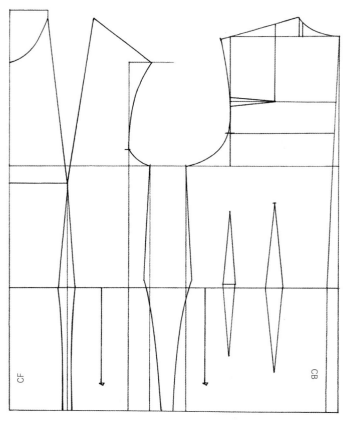

1

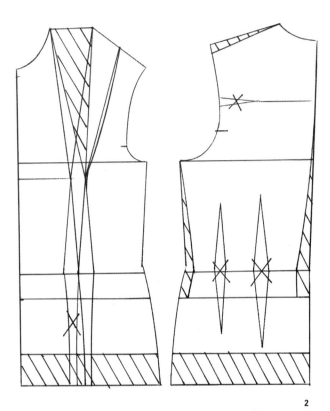

2

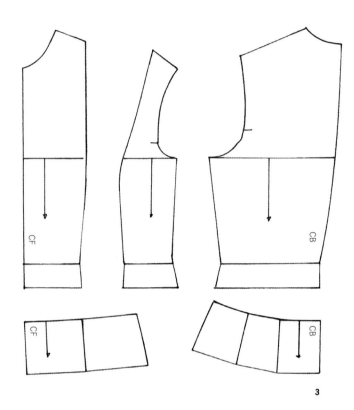

3

2. Starting with the basic sleeve pattern on page 68, draw the shoulders with the desired width and height. Use the waist and hip lines for orientation. Since leather scratches easily, remove the darts on this model. Instead use a main or longitudinal seam — what is called a princess seam — in the front piece to elegantly hide the darts.

Place the princess seam 3 cm from the side seam in the front piece to allow enough room for the pockets in the seams.

Take out the shoulder dart from the back piece and reduce this extra amount from the shoulder seam.

3. Cut the prepared front and back jacket pattern pieces from the fabric on the straight grain.

4. The princess seam is highly recommended for incorporating a vertical inserted pocket with a hidden zipper. Attach the inside edge of the pocket to the middle front.

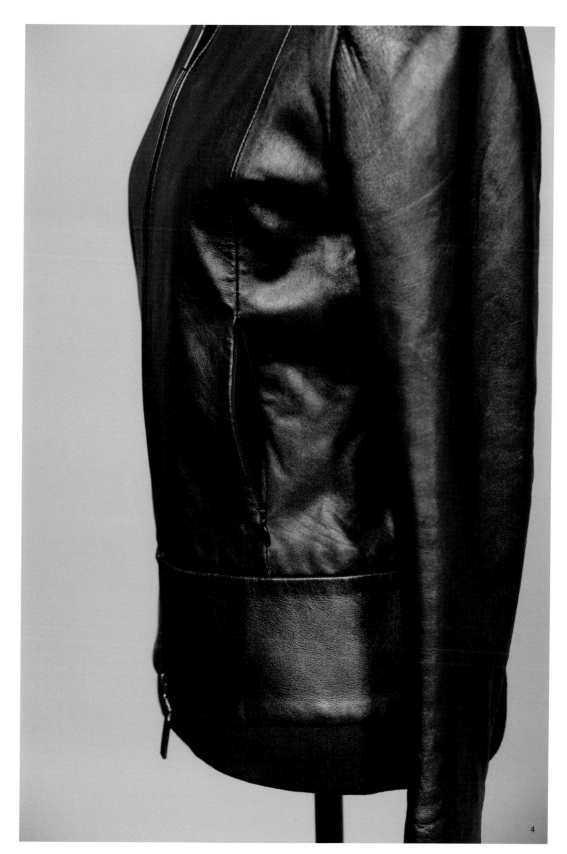

4

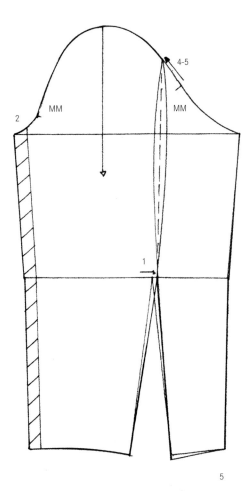

5

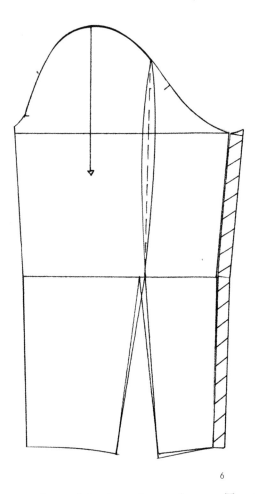

6

5. The sleeve is inspired by the classic double-seamed sleeve, which is narrow and adapts perfectly to this jacket's fitted look.

Make the two pattern pieces then draw a new dart by moving the tip of the dart 1 cm to the right. Extend the lower part of the right side of the sleeve so that the darts are the same length.

Connect the new tip of the dart to a point located approximately 4–5 cm above of the sleeve's back extension. Use this line as a guide for drawing new convex lines for the upper arm. To allow freedom of movement, make these new lines between 0.3 cm and 0.5 cm at the widest point. Separate the sleeve along the new lines of the upper arm at the tip of the dart thereby allowing the dart to be eliminated.

6. The two pieces of the sleeve have to be even. Therefore, bring the inside seam of the sleeve forward by removing a 2 cm-wide strip from it, then add that strip to the seam on the right. Snip the elbow line to make it easier to position.

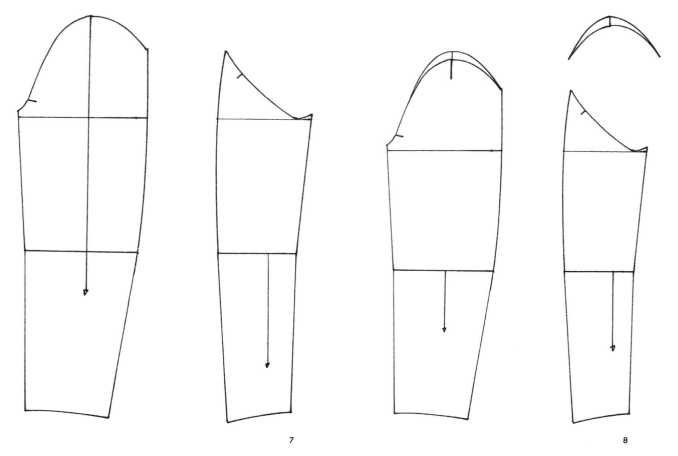

7

8

7. Cut the prepared sleeve pieces from the fabric with the grain, which runs at a straight angle from the elbow line. The sleeve fits well because of the two seams plus the small tuck at the elbow allows it to adjust to the natural shape of the arm, giving the garment maximum comfort.

8. To achieve the special effect in the shoulders, draw a rounded elevation that is added to the jacket shoulders and reinforce the leather with a stiff adhesive lining, cardboard or fine plastic.

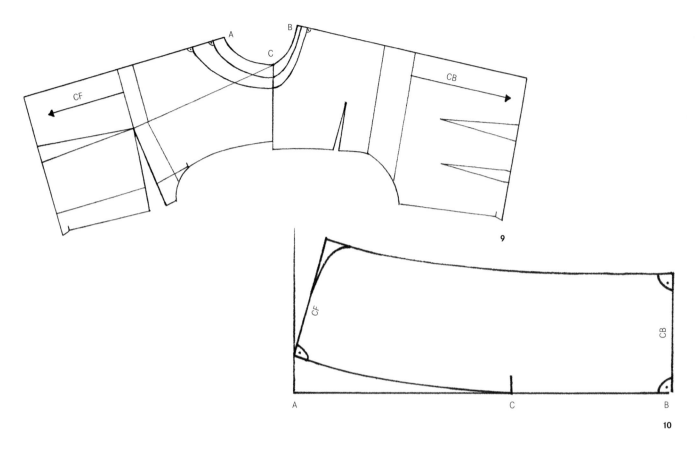

9

10

9. As an embellishment, this model incorporates a raised collar with rounded corners. Make the neck hole wider to accommodate this feature. First, the section that is extended where the neck meets the shoulder seam should be enlarged by no more than half of the center back, otherwise the neck will loosen or slump backwards. It is better to change the cut in the center front.

10. Now make the collar pattern. First, measure the hole for the widened neck from the center front to the center back. Half of that figure is used for the length between end points A and B; point C matches the measured point on the shoulder where the neck rests on the shoulder seam.

Starting with point B, bring the width of the collar up 5 cm for this model, this line forms the center back. Later the collar will be cut separately from this line.

Point A matches the center front. At this point, move the end of the collar up between 1.5 cm and 2 cm along the angle line so that the original collar becomes rounded. This way the jacket collar will fit the rounded neck hole better.

The drawing of the rounded corner of the collar starts at the angled line from upper point A and extends 5 cm for the width of the collar ending at a parallel, slightly oval collar line. Draw a round corner on the collar.

11. A nice detail is the leather zipper with removable two-way closure. The zipper seam is visible and ends at the bottom of the collar.

12. This jacket stands out with its perfect fit and classic style. Nevertheless, working with leather requires specialized acquired knowledge. For this model, a different fabric can be used as long as it is stiff enough, and the neck and sleeve details will have to be reinforced.

BASIC DRESS PATTERN

The basic dress pattern is the foundation for creating dresses and tops but it is also used a lot as the basis for jackets and coats. To create a covering that envelops the body rather than a "second skin," remember to add the following figures to the measurements that you take:

Example in size 10
CC Chest Circumference
92 – 46 – 23 – 11.5 cm
WC Waist Circumference
72 – 36 – 18 cm
HC Hip Circumference
100 – 50 cm

C Collar (1/10 of 1/2 CC + 2 cm)
6.6 cm
BA Back Arc 20.5 cm
BL Back Length 41.8 cm
BL + HD Hip Depth 62.6 cm
CD Chest Depth 28.9 cm
FL Front Length 45.9 cm

BW Back Width 17 cm
AD Armhole Diameter
(1/8 CC % 1.5 cm) 10 cm
CW Chest Width
(1/4 CC % 4 cm) 19 cm

BA Back Arc + 1 cm extra
= 21.5 cm
BW Back Width + 0.5 cm extra
= 17.5 cm
AD Armhole Diameter + 1.5 cm
extra = 11.5 cm
CW Chest Width + 1.5 cm extra
= 20.5 cm
1/2 CC Chest Circumference
(BW + AD + CW) 46 cm +
3.5 cm extra = 49.5 cm
SW Shoulder Width 12.4 cm +
0.5 cm extra from the Back
Width = 12.9 cm front
Shoulder Width, + 0.6 cm extra
width = 13.5 cm back
Shoulder Width CDA
Chest Dart Angle 16°

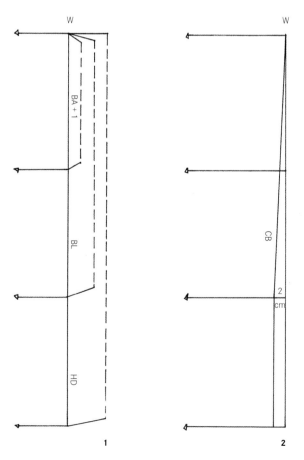

1. Start the pattern by drawing a vertical line downward from the point at the base of the neck (W) with the following measurements: the back arc (21.5 cm + 1 cm extra), the back length and the hip depth (62.6 cm). At each point, draw a right angle to the left for the chest, waist and hip lines.

2. Now, record the curvature of the spine by moving the vertical line 2 cm over at the height of the waistline. From this point, draw a vertical line down over the hip to the hemline and up the back to the point at the base of the neck. This is the center back seam.

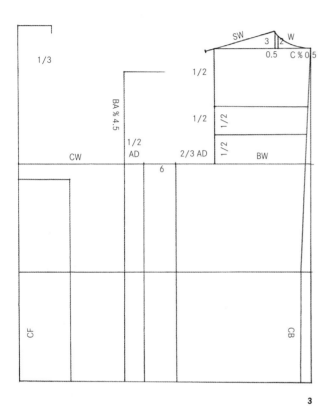

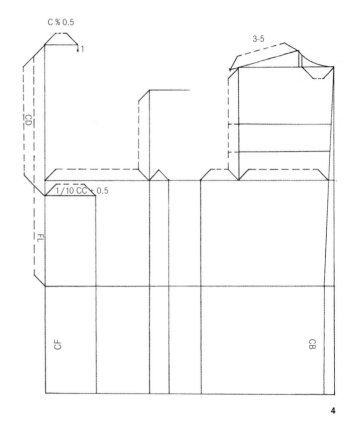

3. Starting from the point where the lines are cut for the center back and the chest, measure the back width towards the left then square up. On the chest line, add 2/3 of the armhole diameter to the left and square down to the hemline. This line will be used later to orient the side seam for the back piece.

Now leave a gap no greater than 6 cm so that there is enough paper to easily separate the front and back pieces later.

From here, measure on the chest line the remaining 1/3 of the armhole diameter. The vertical line at this point is called the front sleeve line.

Now add the width of the chest to the chest line to reach the center of the front piece.

To be on the safe side, stop here briefly and take a test measurement. In this case the chest circumference should measure 49.5 cm without the 6 cm gap.

Once the angled lines are in place, start designing the back part of the neck. Measure the entire neck from the point at the base of

the neck % 0.5 cm. In other words, 6.1 cm towards the left then square up 2 cm and join both points to form a line.

At 0.5 cm to the left, draw a 3 cm parallel line to the back part of the neck then connect this point to the center neck using a French curve.

The back shoulder line also begins at the point where the neck starts. From here, measure the shoulder width to the back's outer point, but keep in mind that the back shoulder seam is 0.6 cm longer than the front seam. Do not trim this difference as it gives a better fit after the shoulder seams are joined.

To determine the position of the back darts, horizontally divide the back rectangle in two. The upper area includes the back arc to the point at the base of the neck. The back sleeve insertion point is located on the lower back area.

For the front shoulder, vertically measure on the front sleeve line the back arc % 4.5 cm — in this case 17 cm — and square to the right a guide line of approximately 10 cm.

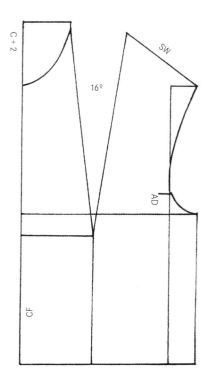

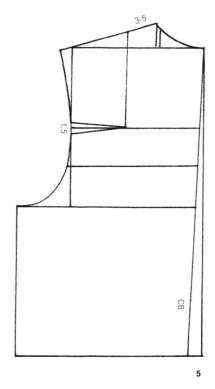

5

4. From the waist at center front, measure upwards the length of the front. Now square to the right the neck measurement % 0.5 cm and from here, square down 1 cm. The left side of the chest dart starts here.

Return to center front and measure down the chest depth, then square to the right 1/10 of the chest circumference adding 0.5 cm.

5. From the highest point on the center front, use the neck measurement adding 2 cm and measure down to get the front part of the neck. Now round off the neckline.

Draw the left side of the chest dart up to its highest point along the angle corresponding to the garment size, in this case 16º. The right side has the same length.

Now join the 12.9 cm front shoulder to the angled dart line and mark the sleeve hole. To get the front insertion mark for the sleeve, on the front sleeve line measure up from the chest line 1/4 of the armhole diameter.

In the upper back area, mark the 1.5 cm wide dart on the back armhole then round off the armhole. Keep in mind that the two shoulder lines join the curvature of the sleeve hole at right angles. If not, unsightly peaks appear when the pieces are sewn together.

That finishes the neck and shoulder areas. The entire basic pattern is drawn according to the measurements of the chest circumference.

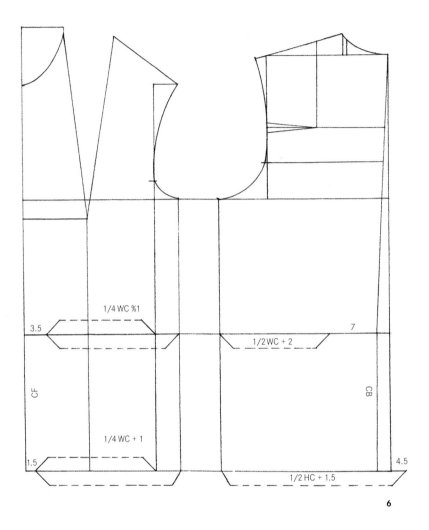

6

6. Keeping in mind differences in body circumferences from person to person, insert darts to reduce the waist and add volume to the curve of the hip.

On the waist line of the front piece, measure 1/4 of the waist circumference % 1 cm to the left of the front sleeve line. From here measure the remaining distance to the center of the front piece. This amount, in this case 3.5 cm, is reduced by the darts.

Calculate the amount for the darts on the hip line by adding 2 cm to the waist formula, which is 1/4 of the waist circumference % 1 cm. In this case, the final amount is 19 cm and the remaining distance to center front is 1.5 cm.

Now mark the darts on the back piece. First, measure to the right of the left outer line 1/2 of the waist circumference, add 2 cm then measure the remaining distance to the center of the back piece, in this case 7 cm. At the hip line, measure to the right 1/2 of the hip circumference and add 1.5 cm; finish by adding the remaining 4.5 cm.

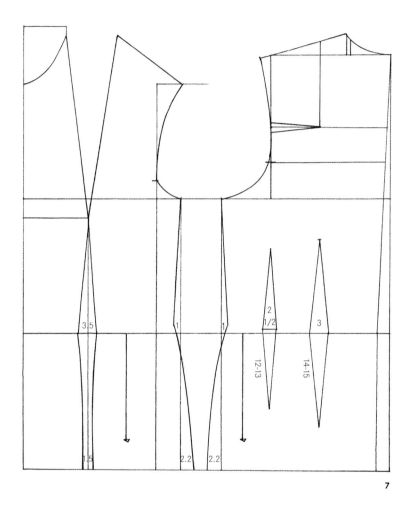

7

7. Here we see the distribution of the surplus fabric and the position of the darts. The front piece dart is located on the line that passes under the highest point on the chest. It is 3.5 cm wide at the waist and 1.5 cm at the hips. From the waistline, draw slightly rounded darts so that they match the body's growing convex shape.

The surplus for the back piece amounts to 7 cm at the waist and 4.5 cm at the hips. This is distributed between the side seams and the two darts so that the pattern perfectly matches the shape of the body. For a better fit, the back darts are not wider than 3 cm.

The body's furthest point coincides with the darts that are close to the side seam. As in the basic skirt pattern, place the widest point of the dart 0.5 cm above the waistline.

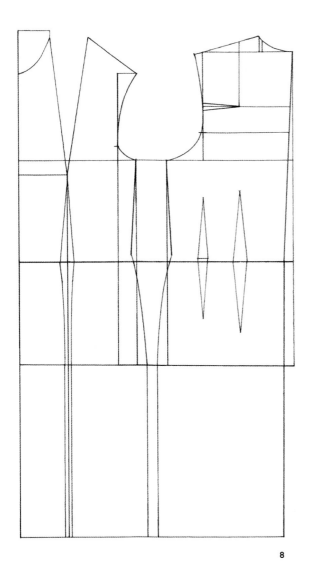

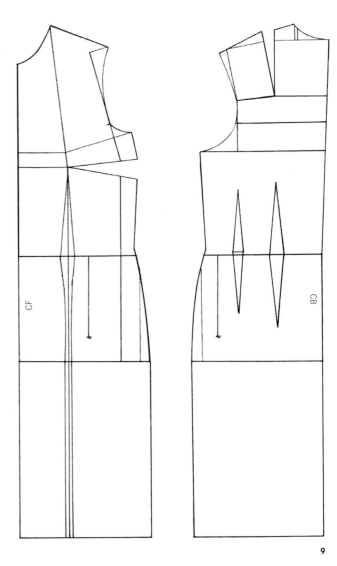

8

9

8. We recommend moving the back armhole dart to the shoulder, and the front chest dart to the side seam, so that the seams are less annoying to the eye and the rest of the cut, such as the neck.

Before cutting, shorten the chest darts and the waist for the front piece by approximately 2 cm so that they do not end right at the chest point.

9. This drawing shows the dress pattern pieces ready for cutting. Whenever you change the location of a seam or dart, always keep in mind that the greater the distance from the original position, the greater the risk to the tailoring.

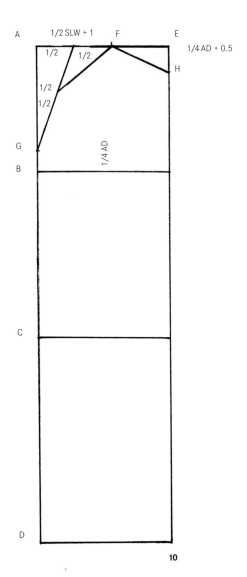

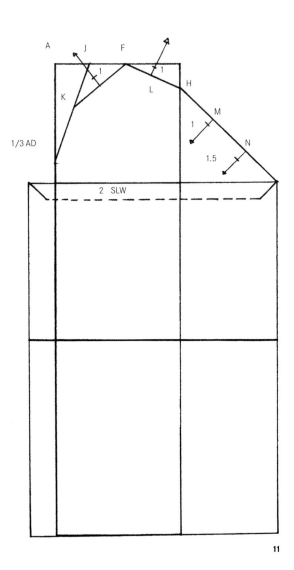

10

11

10. First, draw a vertical line 60 cm long, which is the length of the sleeve. This line starts at point A and ends at point D. For point B, measure down from point A the height of the sleeve crown.

Divide section B–D in half then subtract 2 cm to measure from point B to the elbow line at C. For point E, return to point A and measure to the right the width of the sleeve. Point F, the highest point of the sleeve, is in the middle of section A–E + 1 cm to the

right. When the sleeves are added, this point matches the bodice shoulder seam.

For point G, the front sleeve insertion point, use 1/4 of the armhole diameter and measure straight up from point B. For point H, another design support point, use 1/4 of the armhole diameter plus 0.5 cm and measure straight down from point E.

BASIC SLEEVE PATTERN

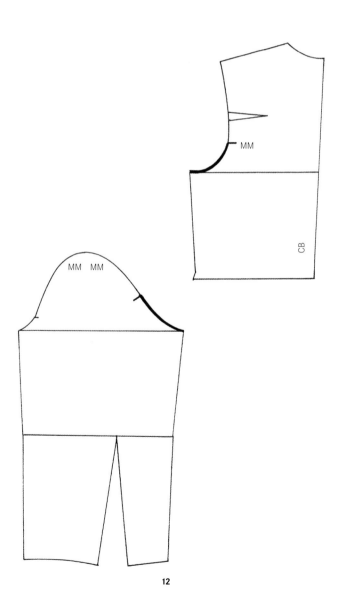

Example in size 10
SL Sleeve Length 60 cm
SDH Sleeve Dome Height
(BA Back Arc % 5.5 cm) 15.5 cm
SLW Sleeve Width (AD
Armhole Diameter + extra 5 cm)
16.5 cm
SEW Sleeve Edge Width 23 cm

BA Back Arc + 1 cm extra =
21.5 cm
AD Armhole Diameter + 1.5 cm
extra = 11.5 cm

The basic sleeve pattern is a classic straight sleeve with one seam. While barely noticeable in the final product, this pattern can be used as the base for almost every type of sleeve, including the two-seamed sleeve, raglan sleeve and batwing sleeve. Since the sleeve is a movable piece that should look stylish when it is moving or hanging at rest, its proper tailoring and finishing is not that easy to accomplish and requires practice.

11. For the sleeve's left seam, use 1/3 of the armhole diameter and measure horizontally to the left of point B. From this new point measure to the right twice the sleeve width, which is the sleeve circumference, to mark the sleeve's right seam.

Now, accurately mark the curving contour of the sleeve crown by determining three support points. From point F, the sleeve's upper insertion point, draw a line to support point H, and divide this line in half for point L. From here, square up 1 cm to meet the line between points F and E.

For point J, divide section A–F in half. Join point J to point G, the front insertion point, and divide this section G–J in half for point K. Join point K to the sleeve insertion point F and square up 1 cm in the middle of section K–F.

For the last two support points draw a line from point H to the right side seam then divide this into three to find starting points M and N. From point M, square down 1 cm and from point N square down 1.5 cm. Use a French curve to draw the rounded sleeve crown.

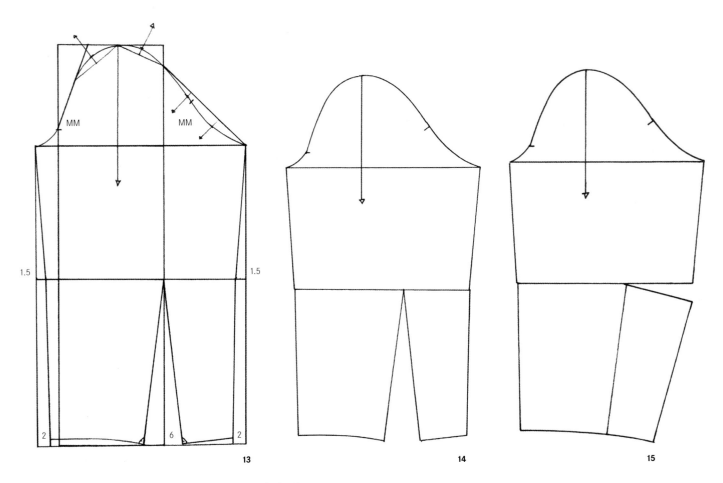

13

14

15

12. Calculate the exact position of the sleeve's back insertion mark by measuring on the bodice the back armhole from the side seam to the sleeve's insertion point. Now add 1 cm and mark the sleeve location.

With the measuring tape, measure the length of the crown from the sleeve's front insertion point to the back point and compare this to the matching areas on the front and back pieces.

There is an intentional difference in sleeve width of approximately 10%, which should be kept when sewn so that the sleeve hangs better.

13. Prepare 1.5 cm side seams for the elbow line. Use 2 cm seams at the wrist for the desired wrist width and to give the sleeve a nice shape that follows the arm circumference.

Now, measure the width of the bottom. The difference between that measurement and the desired wrist width is the amount for the dart. Deduct this from the elbow line and distribute uniformly to the left and right on line E.

Draw a slanted line from the right side of the dart to the side seam to recover the right-angled wrist. Trim the side seams by a few millimeters and fold them towards the sides of the dart.

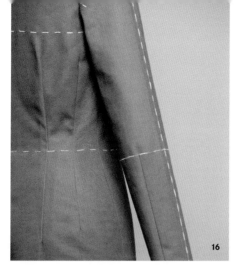

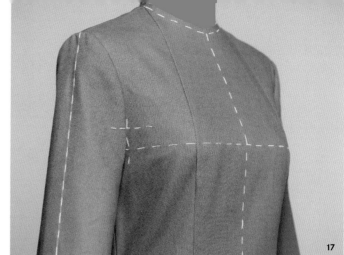

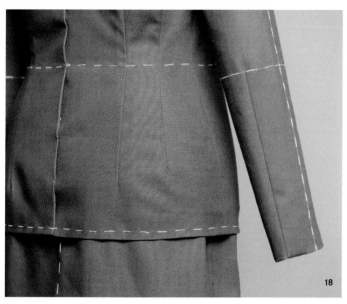

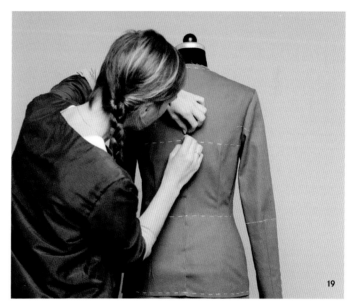

14. This is the prepared one-seamed sleeve with a dart at the wrist.

15. The dart can also be placed and sewn at the elbow line of the back side seam. The advantage to this variation is that the dart is much shorter and, therefore, less noticeable.

16-17. When placing the sleeve, the insertion points should match. Nevertheless, it is not uncommon that the sleeve may need to be placed a bit further forward or further back during the fitting so that the garment fits the individual's body posture. You can also correct the shoulder width this way.

18-19. The darts on the front and back pieces allow the garment to fit the body perfectly. Still, it is often necessary to individually alter the shape of the shoulders, the curve of the back, the waist and the chest.

SLEEVELESS DRESS
WITH FULL SKIRT

1. This dress is based on the basic dress pattern but with a symmetrical gathered upper part and a full skirt. A drawstring joins the front to the back piece and also functions as an adjustable strap. This design needs a fabric that hangs well.

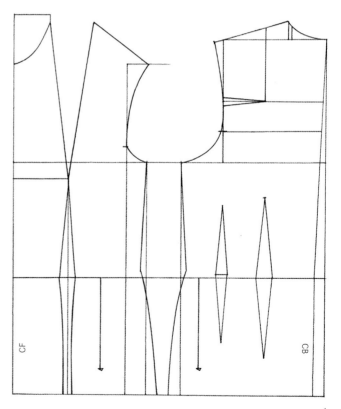

1

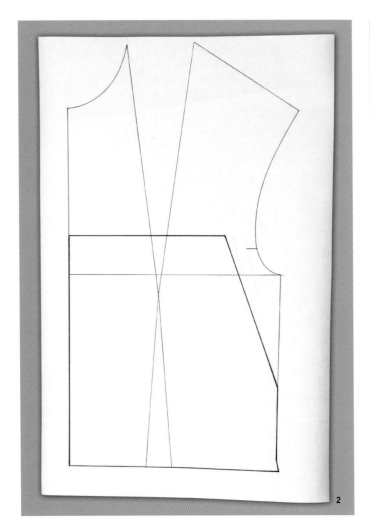

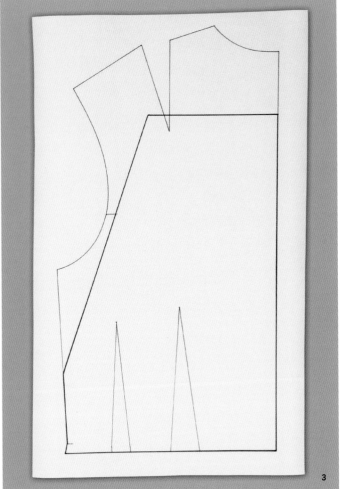

2. Nevertheless, for the upper part the basic dress pattern can only be used to the waistline. The height of the cut and the depth to the arm are easy to figure out but the front piece requires a set minimum height. Use the chest line and the shoulders as guidelines and test the measurements directly on the body.

3. As with the front piece, the basic dress pattern is used to position the back piece. Its shape and height can be different from the front piece but the length of the side seams joining both parts must be the same.

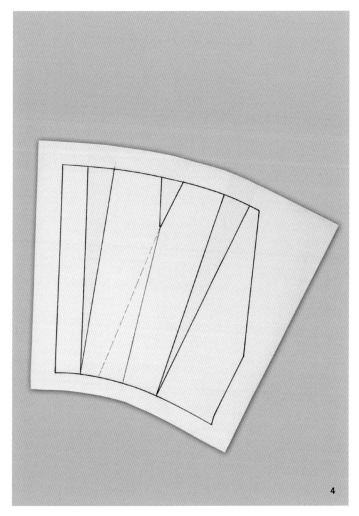

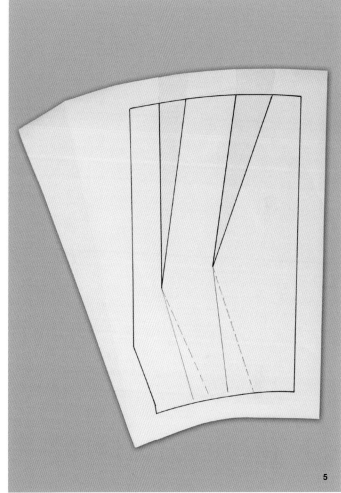

4. The gathered folds indicate extra volume is added to the pattern piece so that the dress can be slipped off later with the help of a drawstring. For the extra amount, cut and open darts.

Place the chest dart and the waist dart on the front piece at the chest point. Here, the waist dart can be moved to the upper edge of the cut. Cut a piece of the chest dart, add the waist dart and the amount needed can be found in the cut.

Next, make two cuts to the left and to the right of the chest dart to gain more volume, and gather it. To even off the corners, give a slight curve to the waistline and the neckline, which are the edges of the cut.

5. In the back piece, draw guidelines from the dart points to the upper edge of the neckline and divide the neckline in three for more volume. Cut these guidelines and add them to the waist darts by joining each piece. This creates the cut's extra volume. Place any extra paper under the front piece.

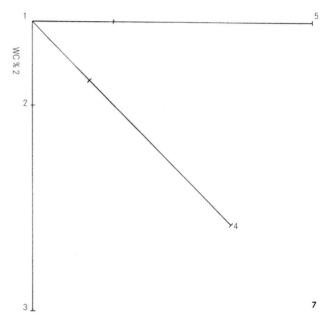

6. The pleated folds on the upper piece have a soft fall because they are sewn on the diagonal. The drawstring on the shoulders is adjusted with a bow.

7. The lower part of the dress consists of a full skirt made with circular arcs. The upper circular arc is needed for the amount at the waist and the second arc for the amount at the edge of the skirt. The following example shows how to prepare the semicircle skirt.

Starting from point 1, draw a long vertical line to the right and another line at a 45-degree angle.

For point 2, measure 1/3 of the waist circumference % 2 cm from point 1 in both directions. If the waist circumference is 68 cm, the corresponding value for point 2 is 20.66 cm. Draw the desired length of the skirt, here 50 cm, from point 2 to point 3.

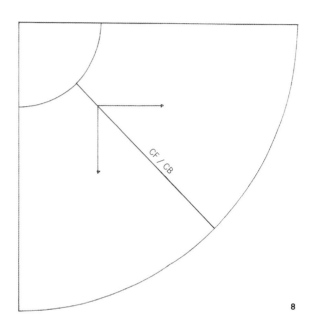

CF / CB

8

9

8. Draw two circular arcs from point 1. If you are working with drawings to scale, you will need a compass. If, on the other hand, you are using the original size, use a metric tape or a piece of drawstring that is adjusted with one hand at the pivot point while with the other draws the circular arc. The sketch drawn represents half of the skirt and can be used for the front piece as well as for the back since both are identical. The line from point 1 to point 4 is the front center and the back center. The lines from point 1 to point 5 and from point 1 to point 3 are the side seams and the thread guide. Therefore, the front and back centers are placed on the diagonal thread guide.

9. The folds fall in a soft regular way because of the significant volume and the diagonal cut. An inconvenience is that the diagonal thread can be seen in the waist area because the fabric stretches a bit. Therefore, before sewing the upper piece, test the waist circumference and establish the desired measurement with a permanent tape.

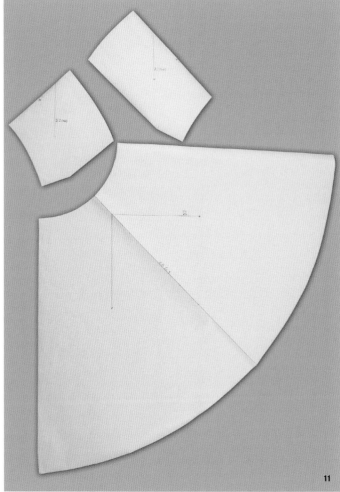

10. For help in drawing the large circular arc, use a metric tape or a piece of string.

11. The finished pieces of the upper part are cut on the diagonal whereas the skirt piece is placed following the grain so that the front and back centers are laid out obliquely at a 45 degree angle.

12. The combination of folds with the full skirt and gathers gives a nice effect to this charming dress.

12

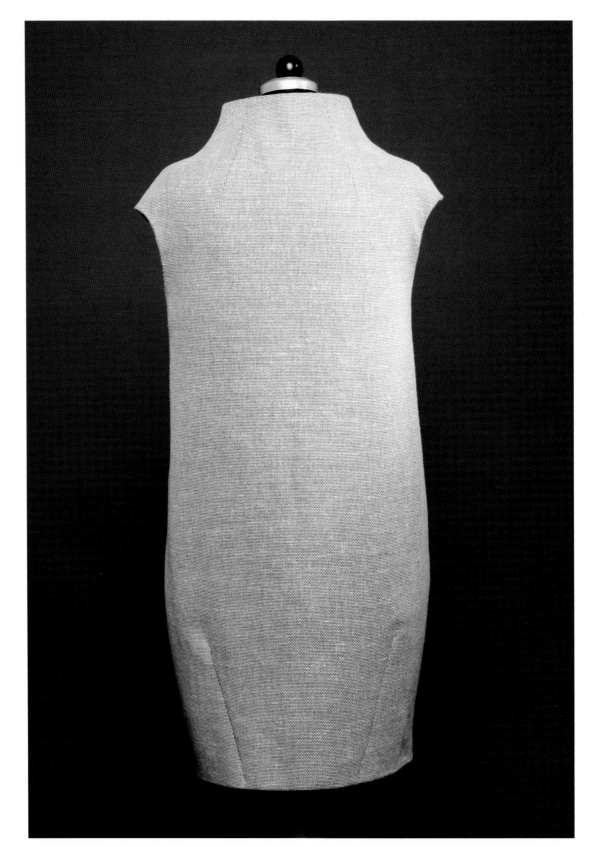

DRESS WITH OVAL SILHOUETTE

1. Unlike the previous model with its soft draping lines, this dress has a static shape. It expresses a truly personal style with its oval silhouette, raised neckline, oblique darts and small seamless sleeves that barely cover the shoulders.

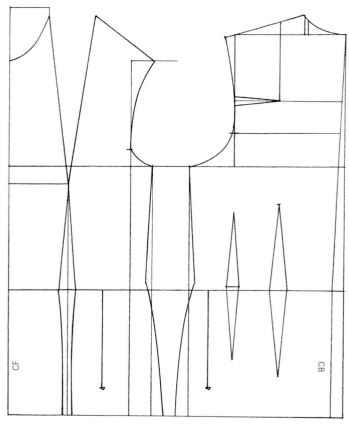

CF

CB

1

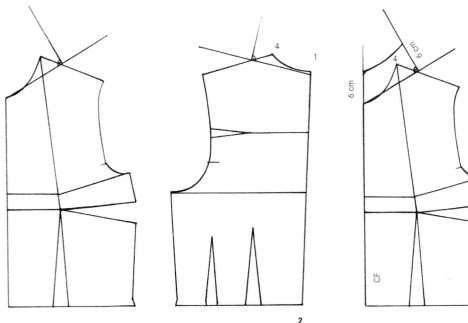

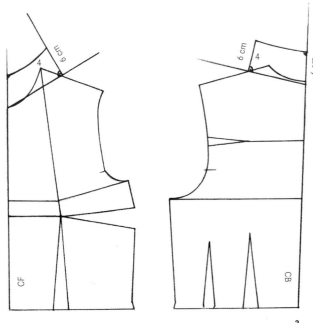

2. Make the opening for the head first before starting the work on the raised neckline. On the basic model, find the point that is 1 cm down from the top of the back and another that is 4 cm away from the neck on the shoulder seam. Join the new points with a straight line, which will create a right angle at the point on the shoulder in the next step.

3. Now draw a 6 cm line at a right angle to the newly created line, and extend the center front and back lines by 6 cm. Use a French curve to draw the new neckline.

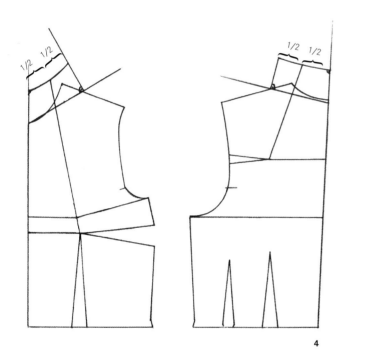

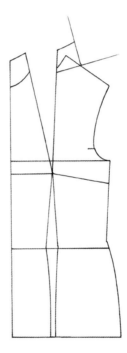

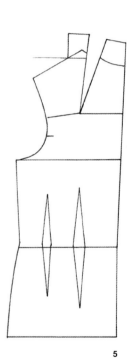

4

5

4. On the new neck edge, determine the center at 1/4 of the neckline then draw a line down to the dart point. This creates the cutting lines and the sides of the darts.

5. For aesthetic reasons, move the chest dart in the front piece and the shoulder dart in the back armhole to the neck area. As shown in figure 5, trim the new cutting lines and place the original darts on them for the new neckline. Reinforce these newly created areas with paper.

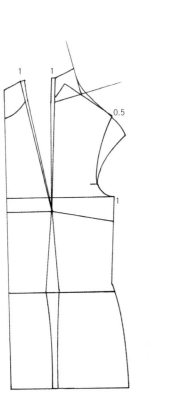
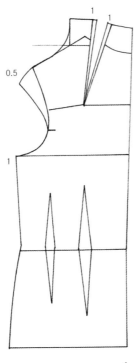

6. For a nicely rounded neckline, include extra margins in the neck and chest areas. To do so, reduce the dart width by 1 cm on one side and add 1 cm to the other side.

Outline the cut sleeves in the armhole. For a close fitting design, draw the shoulder tip with a slight curve of 0.5 cm. Add 1 cm to the armhole so that it does not constrict too much under the arm.

7-8. The shoulder lines should be the same length and shape so that the front and back pieces join easily. The simplest way to ensure this is by taking measurements of the shoulder lines. You can also create a template of the back piece then use it for the front. This dress is easy to put on and take off; finish it with an invisible zipper on the left side.

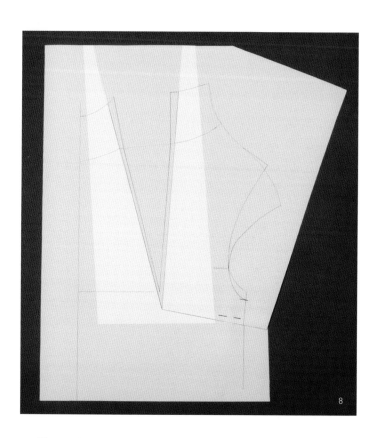

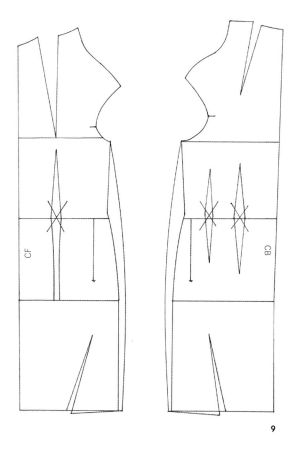

9. To produce the oval shaped silhouette for this dress, extend the basic pattern as much as you want then draw a rounded side seam. Ignore the waist darts since this dress is not fitted.

However, include darts on the hemline for visual symmetry. These darts highlight the garment's round profile. You are free to choose their lengths and positions.

Always remember to compare and adjust the two sides of the darts to avoid problems later when sewing. In this case, the side of the dart that is closest to the center is significant as it determines the length; because of its diagonal placement, it juts out from the original edge. To adjust this, just create a new right angle at the corner of the side seam.

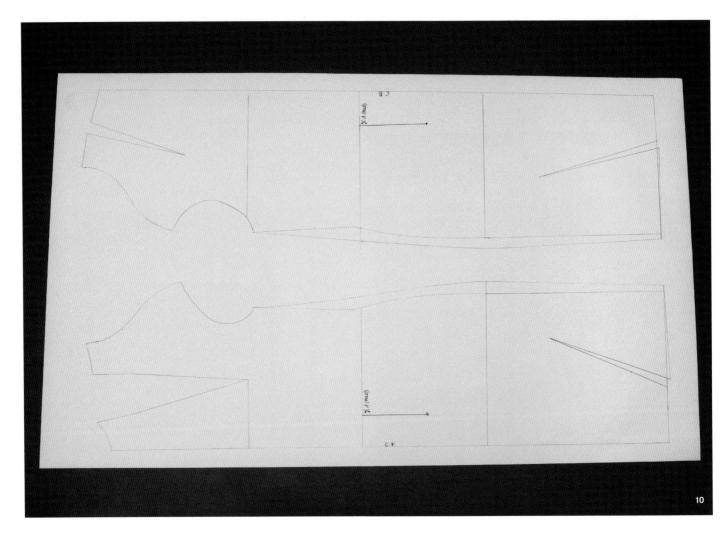

10. These are the finished cutting pieces: in this model the center front and center back are separate.

11. The cut of the sleeves, and the neckline raised up and away from the neck, give a distinctive flair to this dress. Use a fabric with some thickness for this model, and reinforce the neck and shoulder areas as well as the dress hemline with lining.

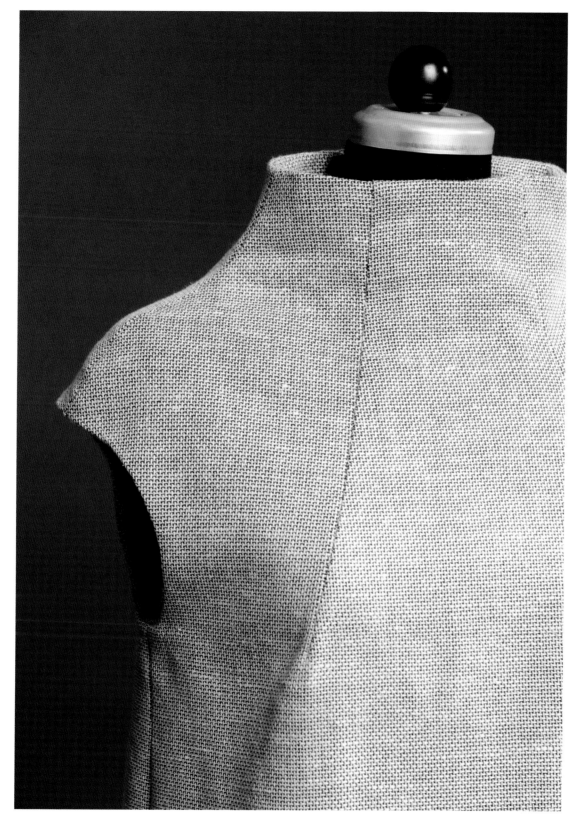

THE TIGHT DRESS

What really stands out about this fitted garment designed by Leyre Valiente is the use of different overlapping pieces. To set them apart, use fabrics with contrasting textures. Another striking element is the ruffles on the sleeves. Simplify the task by using pleated satin, which is available in a large variety of colors and sizes.

This is a dress with many pieces so you have to be very careful when it comes to choosing the fabrics and beads. It is important that all of the elements stand out yet you must resist the overly ornate.

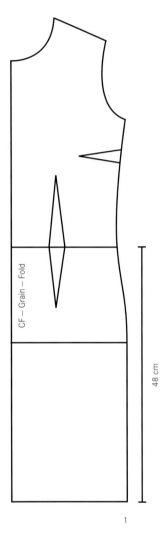

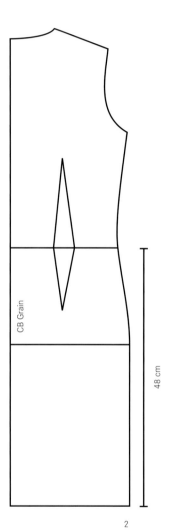

1. Use the basic pattern for the front length with the skirt measurement of 48 cm for the length. Cut this pattern piece once on the fold using silk satin, or a fabric with a similar texture, and once with the lining.

2. Now take the basic pattern for the back length and add the same length as in the front. This time cut the pattern piece twice in wool voile and twice in lining. These two pattern pieces form the foundation for this dress.

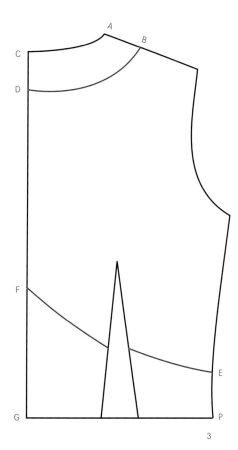

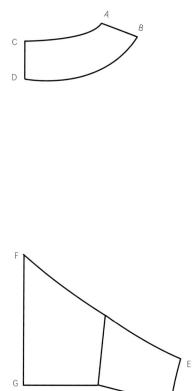

3. Use a basic back pattern piece for the outfit's second layer. Draw a curve from D to B that is 4 cm from line C–A. The point F is located 14 cm up from G, and E is 4.8 cm up from P. Draw a curve from F to E. Cut the pattern piece along these two curves and close the dart.

4. Set aside the resulting upper and lower pattern pieces; they will be used later with the altered front piece.

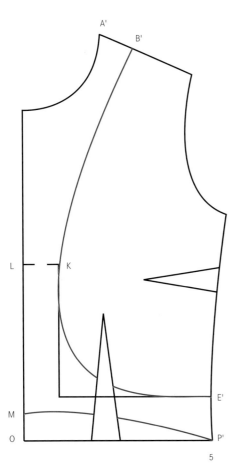

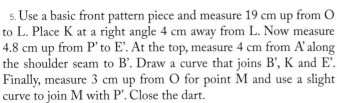

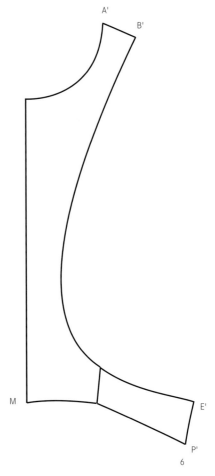

5. Use a basic front pattern piece and measure 19 cm up from O to L. Place K at a right angle 4 cm away from L. Now measure 4.8 cm up from P' to E'. At the top, measure 4 cm from A' along the shoulder seam to B'. Draw a curve that joins B', K and E'. Finally, measure 3 cm up from O for point M and use a slight curve to join M with P'. Close the dart.

6. Cut the pattern piece along the curves from B'–E' and from M–P'. This piece will be joined to the two pieces that were put aside earlier in step 4.

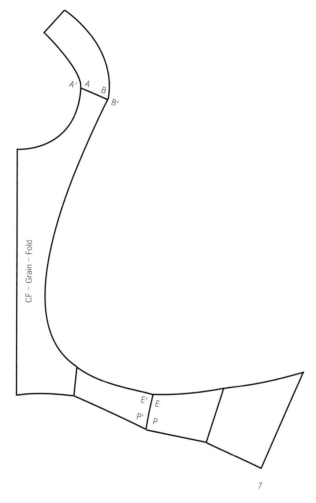

CF – Grain – Fold

A' A B
B'

E' E
P' P

7

7. To join the three pattern pieces, connect the lines A–B to A'–B' and E'–P' to E–P. Cut this pattern piece on the fold, once in black silk satin and once in the lining.

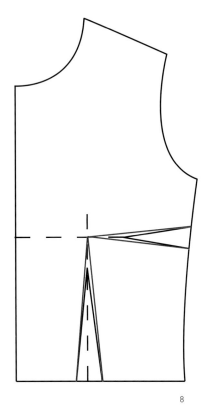

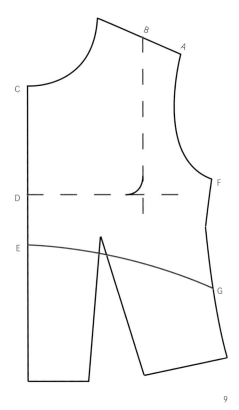

8. Finally, use another basic front pattern for the vest. Extend the centers of the darts until they meet then close the chest dart but keep the fitted bodice dart.

9. From A at the tip of the shoulder, measure 6 cm to point B. From C on the center line, measure 13 cm down to point D. Connect D to B with right-angled lines but curve the intersecting point slightly. From D, measure down 6 cm to point E and from F, measure down 13 cm to G. Now join E to G with a curved line. Cut the pattern piece along the lines D–B and E–G.

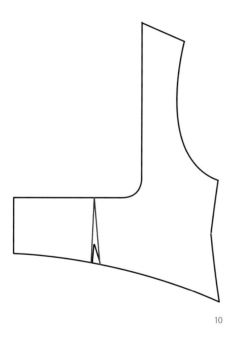

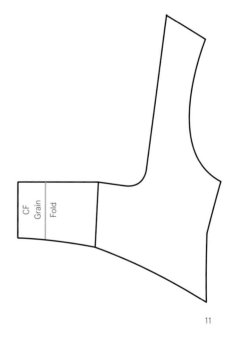

10

11

10. Lengthen the dart on the pattern piece by extending the tip to the other side of the pattern. Now close the altered dart.

11. Cut the resulting pattern piece once with the black silk satin fabric and once with the lining. Remember, the word "fold" on the pattern means the fabric should be doubled when cut.

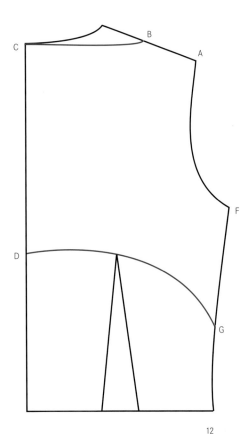

12

13

12. Now take another basic back pattern. From A, measure 6 cm to point B; join B to C with a slight curve. From C, measure down 22 cm to D and from F, measure down 13 cm to G; join D to G with a curve that passes right over the tip of the dart.

13. Cut this pattern piece twice with the black silk satin and twice with the lining.

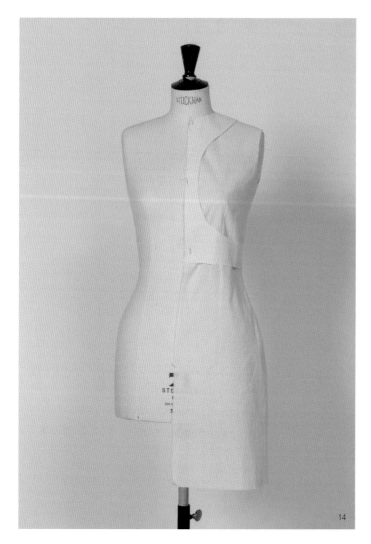

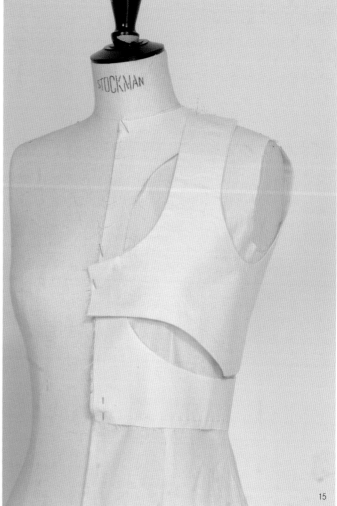

14. To assemble the outfit, begin by placing the two foundation pattern pieces from steps 1 and 2 on a mannequin. Then place the pieces from step 7 for the second layer on the mannequin and try to align them with the underlying dress.

15. Finally, assemble the removable vest that adds versatility to the dress. If sleeves are desired, cut as many rectangles and layers as needed from the pleated silk using the length of the armhole then sew these pieces to the armhole.

DRESS WITH ONLY ONE SEAM
AND RIBBON FRINGES

This is a slightly fitted garment with a single seam at the back where the zipper goes. The key element is the organza ribbons and the fabric for this dress has been chosen with this in mind. Silk is the perfect canvas for this work of art as it is soft to the touch and has a clean line.

Since the ribbons define this garment's character, choose colors that agree with the wearer's personality. Decide if the colors should be warm or cool, or maybe use a monochromatic scale.

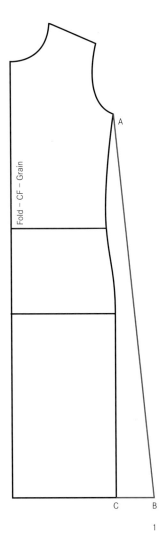

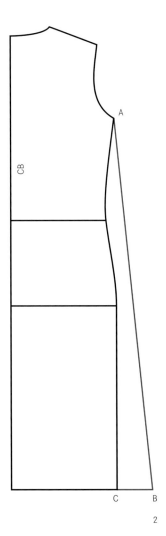

1. For this dress, use basic long pattern pieces as your starting point. First, take a basic front pattern piece and extend the bottom at point C by 8 cm to the right to point B. Use a straight line to join B to A.

2. Now take a basic back pattern piece and repeat step 1. Again, the distance from C to B is 8 cm; join B to A on the back piece.

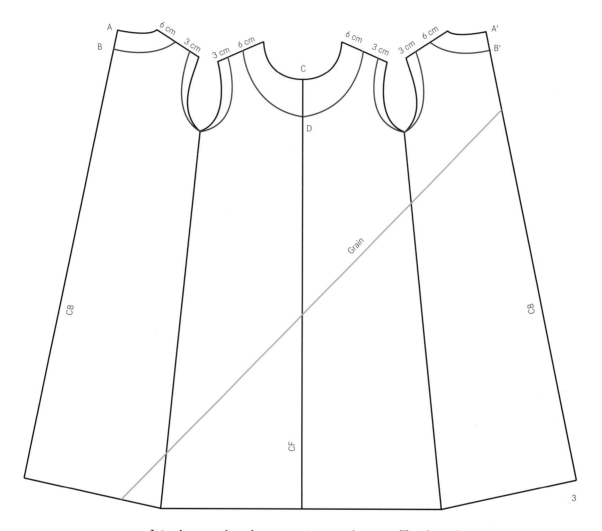

3. Join the two altered pattern pieces at the seam. To adjust the necklines and armholes, measure 5 cm down from points A and A' for points B and B' respectively. For point D, measure 10 cm down from C. Draw the new cutting lines following the measurements in the illustration. Cut this altered pattern piece once in silk and once in the lining.

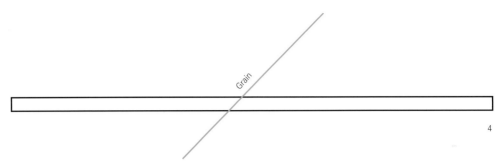

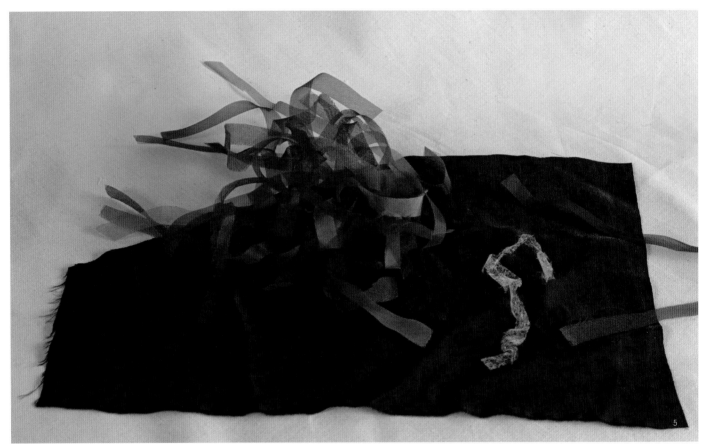

4-5. For the ribbon fringe, cut on the bias several 30 x 1 cm silk organza rectangles in different colors. In this case, we chose a warm color range made up of red, orange, russet and purple.

6

6. To create fringes on the hemline and neckline, join the ribbons together in loops. Place a 1 x 1 cm square of adhesive interfacing between the ribbon and the dress then heat it with an iron so that they stick together.

DRESS WITH ONLY ONE SEAM AND TULLE RUFFLES

This dress with a flared silhouette has been chosen for this book because it is easy to make and it is so flexible. We have used a fabric without a lot of hang since the tulle gives the dress its volume.

Because this pattern is so simple, the dress can be made with a textured fabric and the tulle ruffle will not seem too ornate. For variety, use a smooth fabric with colored tulle.

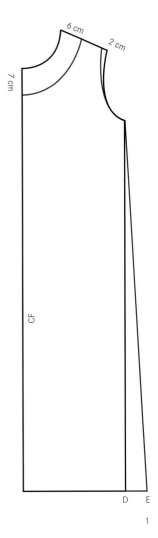

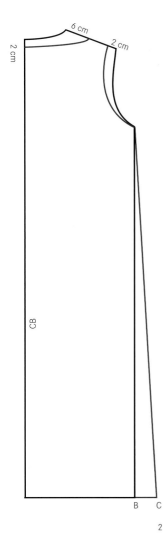

1. Use a long straight basic front pattern piece. First, extend the bottom at point D by 6 cm and flare to the right to point E. Draw a straight line from E to the underarm. Next, lower the neckline on the fold by 7 cm and remove 6 cm from the neckline at the shoulder. Remove 2 cm from the shoulder at the side.

2. Now take the long straight basic back pattern piece and alter it by extending the line at point B by 6 cm to the right to point C. Draw a line from C to the underarm. Next, lower the neckline on the fold by 2 cm and remove 6 cm from the neckline at the shoulder. Remove 2 cm from the shoulder at the side.

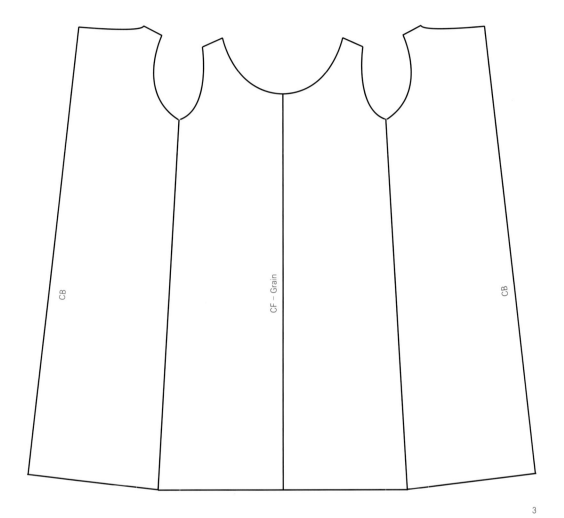

CB

CF – Grain

CB

3

3. Join the two altered pattern pieces at the side seams. Cut this new pattern piece once using the fabric.

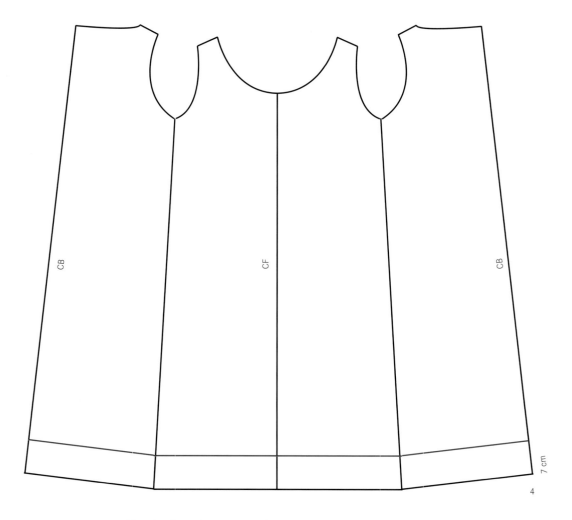

CB

CF

CB

7 cm

4

4. For the dress lining, copy the previous pattern and trim 7 cm
from the hemline. Cut this pattern piece once using the lining.

5

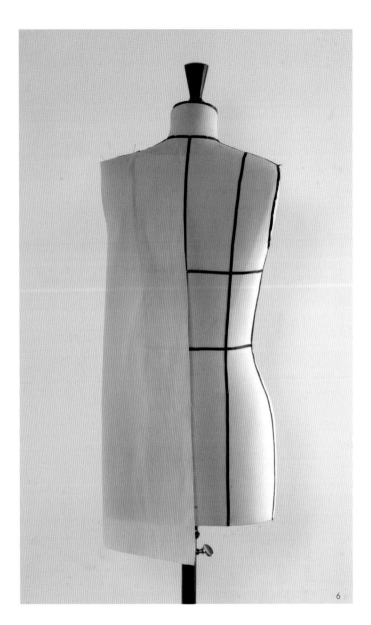

6

5. For the ruffles, draw a 300 × 30 cm rectangle and cut this pattern piece four times in rigid tulle.

6. When you assemble the dress, fit it snugly to the mannequin. Sew the back piece but leave an opening for the invisible zipper. Place the lining under the dress and sew the four tulle rectangles to the hem. For volume, place one rumpled ruffle on top of the other.

DOUBLE DRESS
WITH ONLY ONE SEAM

The uniqueness of this straight dress comes from the fact that it is folded at the bottom without a seam. If the hem is not accentuated the missing seam will probably be overlooked. Here however, it is highlighted with added volume on the inside of the doubled fabric.

The simplicity of this dress turns it into a basic garment that is suitable for day or night depending on the accessories used such as necklaces, purses and shoes.

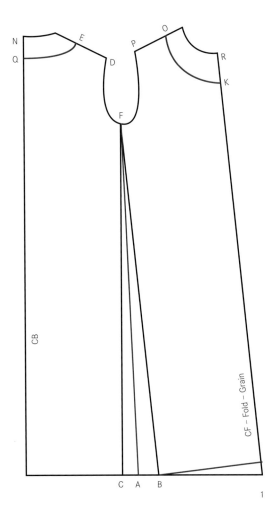

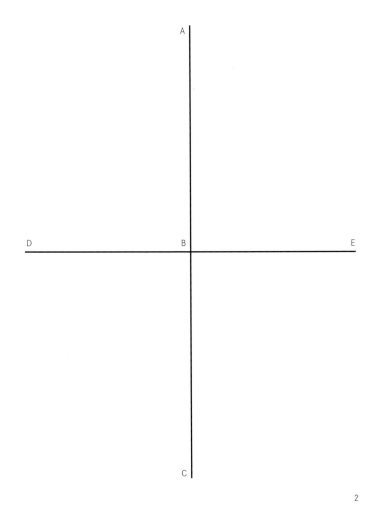

1. Use the straight long basic front and back pattern pieces and join them at point F under the armhole. Pivoting at F, rotate the front piece until the distance from B on the front bottom to C on the back bottom is 7 cm. To alter the front neckline, place point O on the front shoulder 7 cm away from P. For point K, measure 7 cm down from R. Join K and O with a curved line. To alter the back, place point E on the back shoulder 7 cm away from D and point Q on the center back 5 cm down from N. Join Q and E with a curved line. Cut the pattern along these two new lines as in figure 1 and set aside.

2. Now draw a cross. Line A–B measures 200 cm and line D–E is 150 cm; point B is the midpoint for both lines.

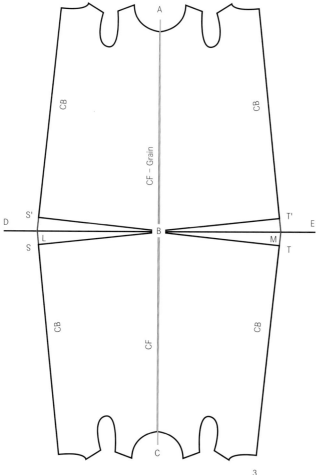

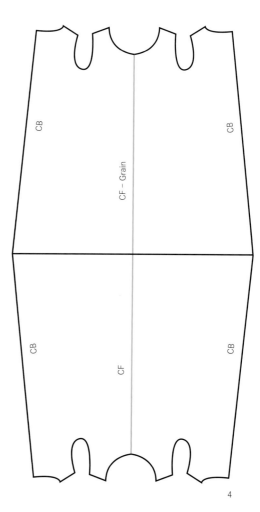

3. Place the pattern on the cross four times so that the center front always matches the vertical axis. Extend the lines at points T and T' until they meet at point M. Repeat the process at points S and S' to get point L. Points L and M rest on line D–E.

4. Place this altered pattern piece on the fabric and cut it once only.

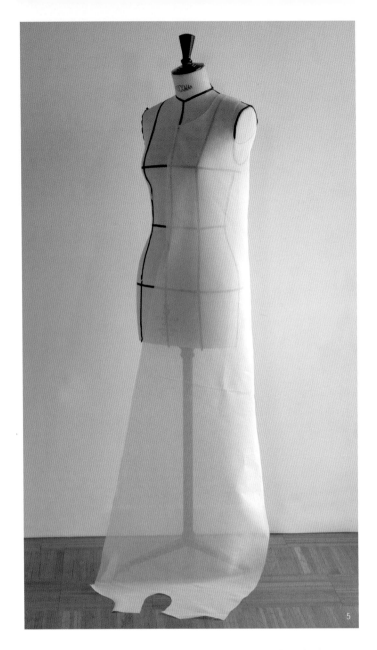

5. Since this dress is made from one piece and only has one seam, its assembly is very simple. First, place the pattern on the mannequin and join the shoulders.

6. Now, fold the pattern in half upwards and join the edges of the neckline, the shoulders and the armholes. Sew the back seam. For added volume, place a few 20 cm wide strips of tulle inside the hem.

6

DRESS WITH BATWING SLEEVES

This dress is designed by Miguel Madriz who recommends using only stretch tulle so that the bodice fits properly. The fabric is characterized by its flexibility and different types are available. The elegant fabric used here has embossed decorations and can be bought at any fabric store.

In addition to volume, this dress plays with transparency. The bodice is made from stretch tulle covered in motifs while the skirt is made from irregularly ballooned layers of tulle that are more see-through in some areas than in others.

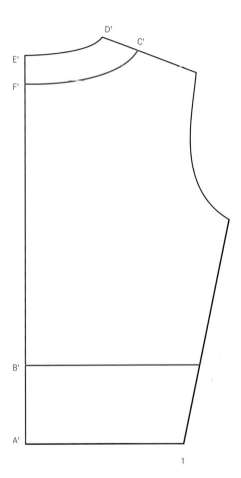

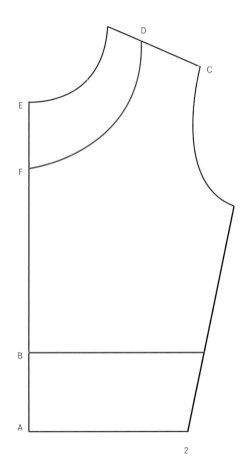

1. Use the basic straight back pattern and shorten it by 8.5 cm from point A' to point B'. For the new neckline, place point C' on the shoulder 7 cm away from D' and point F' on the center back 3 cm down from E'. Use a slight curve to join C' and F'. Set this back pattern piece aside.

2. Now alter the basic straight front pattern. Shorten the pattern piece by 8.5 cm from point A to point B. For the new neckline, follow the original curve and join point D (7 cm from C) to point F (7 cm from E).

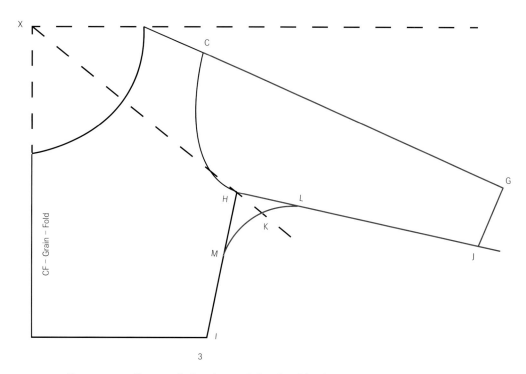

3

3. From point C, extend the slope of the shoulder by 36 cm to reach point G then extend the line down at a right angle. Extend line I-H to the right at a right angle until it intersects the previous line at point J. Draw a line from X to H then add 3.5 cm to reach point K. On the bodice, point M is 7 cm down from H; on the sleeve, point L is also 7 cm from H. Join L and M with a curve that also passes through K. Cut this pattern on the fold once in stretch tulle.

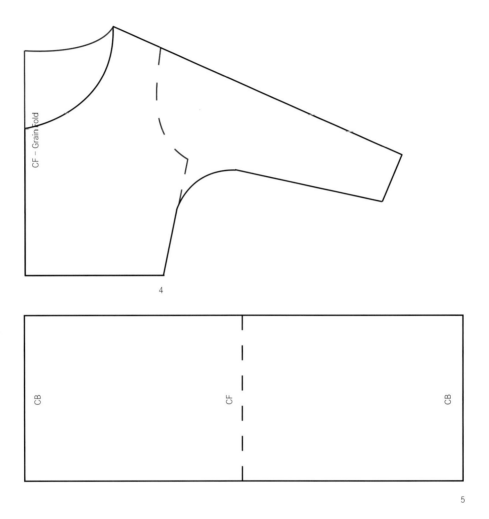

CF – Grain fold

4

CB

CF

CB

5

4. For the back pattern, copy the recently made front pattern piece and place it under the prepared back pattern to fix the neckline. Cut this back pattern piece on the fold once in stretch tulle.

5. For the skirt, draw a 300 cm x 110 cm rectangle and cut it four times in black tulle.

6. Place the front and back pieces on the mannequin and stitch together. Sew the bands of tulle in four layers onto the bodice and gather them for an irregular fit.

7. Once the tulle is sewn, bunch up each layer and tack them into place as show in figure 7.

PLEATED DRESS

This dress is simple to make since it only has one seam. Nevertheless, the pleats can present certain challenges. To ensure the garment remains pleated, at least 20% of the fabric must be synthetic fiber; it cannot be 100% natural. More details can be found in the glossary.

The neckline for this dress is originally made from fabric. For the model shown in the photographs, it is replaced with a necklace of stones encased in fabric that can be sewn to the dress.

1

1. Join as many panels of taffeta as needed to reach a width of 285 cm and iron the resulting seam or seams. Hem the fabric then make 19 pleats, each 5 cm wide. The final width of the pleated fabric will be 95 cm.

2. Use an iron for the pleats so that they are clearly marked on the fabric. Keep in mind that the ideal temperature for ironing taffeta is between 212°F and 320°F (100°C and 160°C).

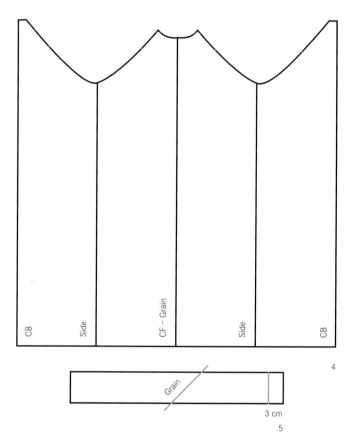

3. Join the basic straight long front and back pattern pieces at the side. To adjust the neckline, from point A, measure 5 cm to point D and from point B measure 3.6 cm to point E. Use a slight curve to join D and E to C where the armholes meet. The resulting pattern piece is for the right side.

4-5. To make the cloth neckline, cut two 41 cm x 6 cm rectangles, one from taffeta and the other from interfacing. These will be folded into a 41 cm x 3 cm rectangle.

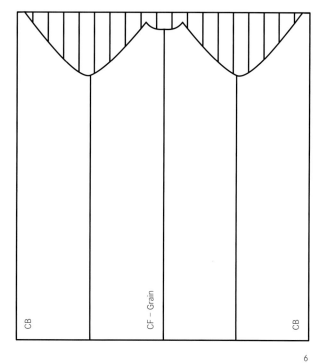

CB

CF – Grain

CB

6

6. Place the pattern on the pleated fabric and cut once. Cut again using the lining. Finally, to achieve this model's flared effect, cut 20 cm wide rectangles of rigid tulle and place them between the dress and the lining in order to expand the garment.

SEMICIRCLE:
THE TRAPEZE DRESS

This model combines concave and convex shapes in one silhouette. It has a very high neckline with slightly fitted shoulders and a loosely hanging body. The bottom piece on the dress has less volume, which makes it comfortable and easier to walk in. It also gives the dress its unusual esthetic.

Each piece of the dress has been made using a different fabric. It is important that all three fabrics have the same texture and weight so that the garment is balanced.

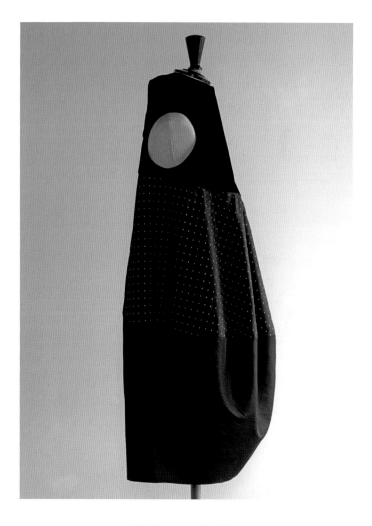

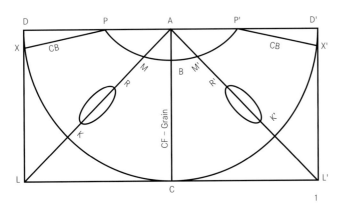

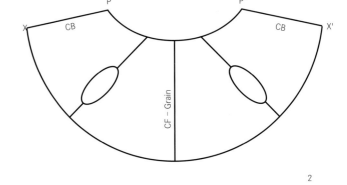

1. For this pattern, begin by making an 82 cm x 41 cm rectangle then divide it into two squares by drawing a line from A to C. From A, draw a semicircle with a 41 cm radius then take the following three measurements from point A: 12 cm down to point B; 18.5 cm to the left for point P; and 18.5 cm to the right for point P'. Join points P, B and P' with a curved line. From point D at the top left corner, measure down 5 cm to point X then join X to P. Repeat at the top right corner with D', X' and P'. Return to point A and draw diagonal lines to L and L'. From point M on line A–L, measure down 11 cm to point R; from point R, measure down 15 cm to K. Join R to K with an oval for the armhole. For the left armhole, repeat on line A–L' with points M', R' and K'.

2. Cut this pattern piece along the line joining X-P-P'-X' then mark it and cut it, once with the selected velvet and once with the lining.

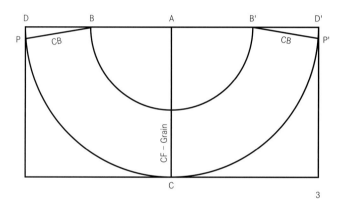

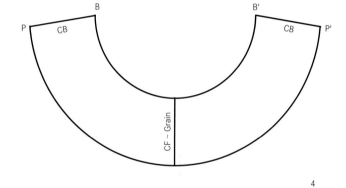

3. Next, draw a 148 cm × 74 cm rectangle then divide it in half by drawing a line from A to C. From the center point A, draw a semicircle with a 41 cm radius to points B to B'. Draw a second semicircle with a 74 cm radius to points D and D'. From point D, measure down 5 cm to point P, then join P and B. Repeat on the right with points D', P' and B'.

4. Cut out the pattern along the line P-B-B'-P' then cut it, once with the selected polka dot fabric and once with the lining.

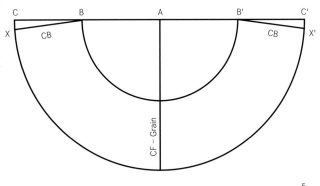

5

6

5. For the bottom piece, from center point A, draw a semicircle with a 40 cm radius and another with a 74 cm radius. From point C, measure down 5 cm to point X then join X to B as in step 3. Repeat this on the right side with points C', X' and B'. Cut the pattern piece along X-B-B'-X' then cut it, once with the taffeta and once with the lining.

6-7. Sew the semicircles in order, starting with the upper part of the dress, which has the armholes. Once this piece is assembled correctly on the mannequin and it has been closed, start on the second piece.

Here you can see the three semicircles, assembled and sewn.

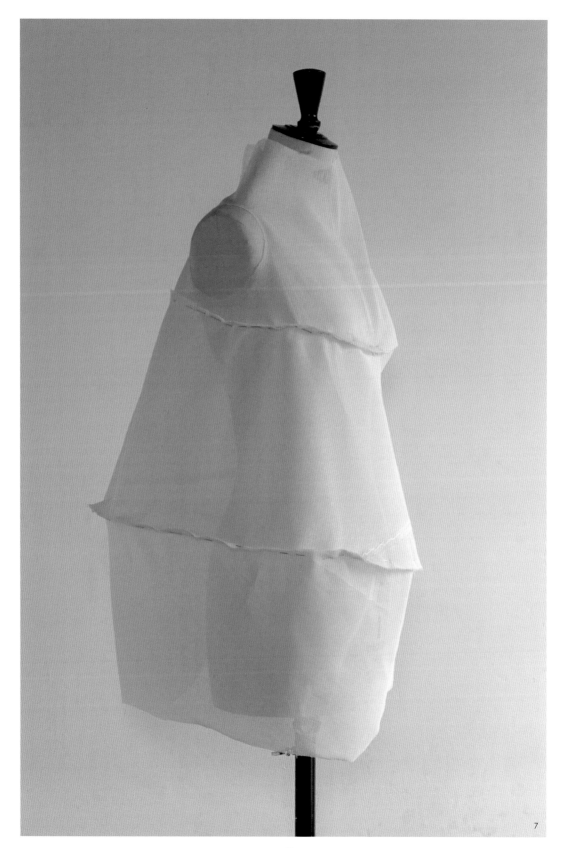

7

CIRCLE:
DRESS WITH HALTER NECK

This type of neckline, high in front and tied at the back of the neck, is popular in evening dresses and bathing suits. It stands out because it is one of the few styles to focus attention on a person's back. This model in particular has the added feature of using only one seam.

In this dress, two silver buckles in a diamond shape are used to fasten the neckline. The features and materials used depend on the style that you want to give the dress.

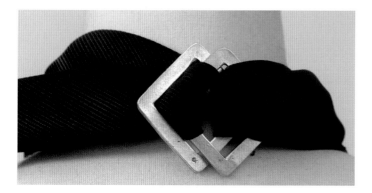

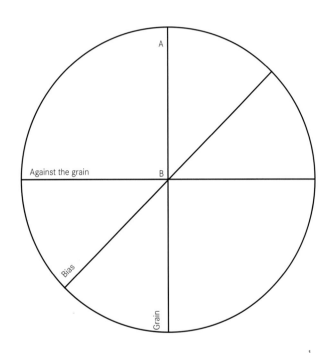

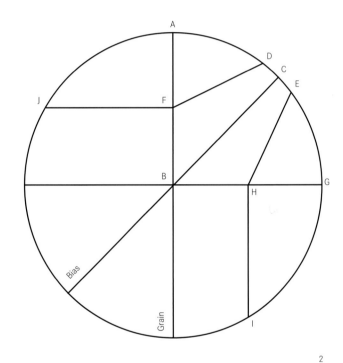

1. Draw a circle with a 75 cm radius, which is the measurement from point A to B; this is the dress length. Now, draw two lines at right angles and another at a 45 degree angle.

2. From point C, measure 8 cm to point D and 8 cm to point E. From point A, measure down 40 cm to point F, and create a perpendicular line to the left that ends at J. Repeat from point G by measuring 40 cm to the left to point H then square down to point I. Cut the pattern piece along the lines E-H-I and D-E-J.

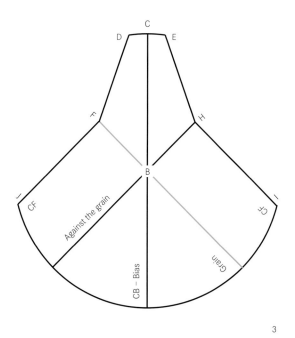

3

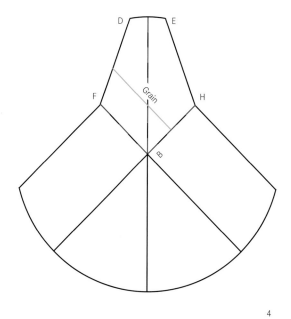

4

3. Once the pattern piece is cut, open it from points C and B then mark it once on the dress fabric and cut it.

4. Join points D, E, H, B and F to make the collar facing pattern. Cut this piece once using the collar facing fabric.

5. To assemble the dress, place the pattern on the mannequin with the opening to the front. At the back, make sure that point B reaches the center back at the height of the waist area as seen in the photograph then fasten it in place.

6. For the front part, sew the dress joining lines F–J with H–I starting from points F and H and moving downward. This is where the invisible zipper goes since this is the only seam on the dress.

7. To shape the neckline, cross one front piece over the other and join both pieces at the back of the neck with the buckles to fasten the dress.

7

CIRCLE:
COCOON SILHOUETTE DRESS

This dress silhouette gets its name because it wraps around the body at the top then expands as it falls away and detaches itself, like a silkworm cocoon. It is made from two circles: one is the inside of the dress itself while the outside acts as a coat.

If the black dress fabric is combined with a printed interior, the latter must have enough black to retain the dignity of a cocktail dress. In this case, the timeless elegance of the black-white combination is used.

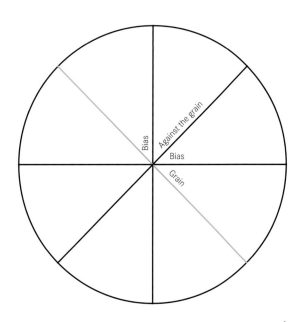

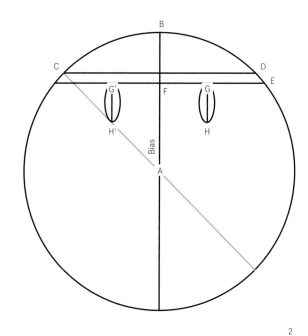

1. This dress has two pieces: one piece is the inside of the dress and the other piece is the outside. This pattern is the inside piece. To start, draw a circle with a 60 cm radius.

2. Perpendicular to line A–B, draw an 86 cm line connecting points C and D. For point E, measure 6 cm from point D then draw a line to the left that is parallel to line C–D. From point F, measure 21 cm on each side for points G' and G. At a right angle to point G, measure 17 cm down to point H. Repeat from G' for point H'. Draw the armholes between G' and H', and G and H. Now, cut the pattern along line C–D.

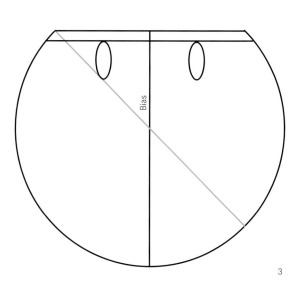

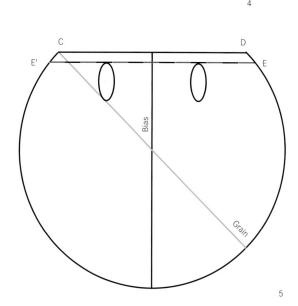

3. This pattern piece is cut once using the black fabric and again using the black fabric with the printed polka dots.

4-5. For this pattern's collar facing, cut along line E'–E and mark it once on the interfacing.

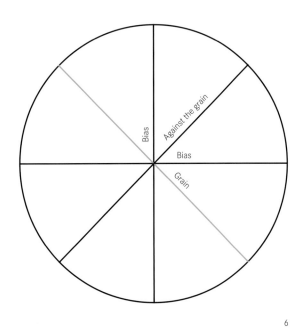

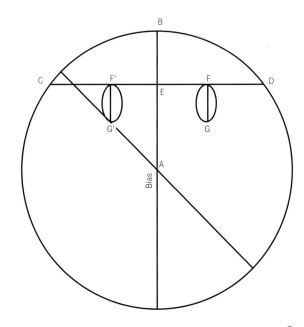

6. Now, prepare the pattern piece for the outside of the dress. As above, draw a circle with a 60 cm radius for the first step.

7. Perpendicular to line A–B, draw a 98 cm horizontal line between points C and D. From center point E, measure 21.5 cm to each side for points F' and F. At a right angle to point F', measure 16 cm down to point G'. Repeat from F down to point G. Draw the armholes between F' and G', and F and G. Now, cut this pattern piece once in the smooth fabric and once in the printed fabric.

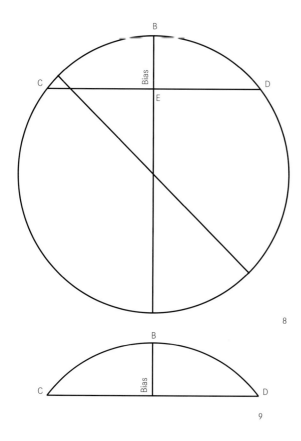

8

B

C

Bias

E

D

B

C

Bias

D

9

C

A

Grain

D

B

10

8-9. Cut the pattern along line C–D. This new pattern piece is the collar facing for the overcoat; mark it on the interfacing and cut once.

10. For the dress ties, draw an 80 cm x 5 cm rectangle and cut it twice out of the fabric.

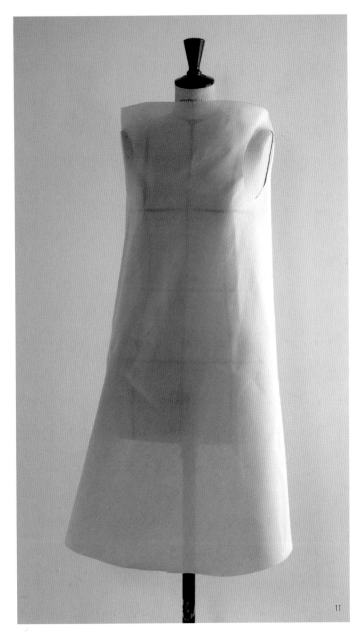

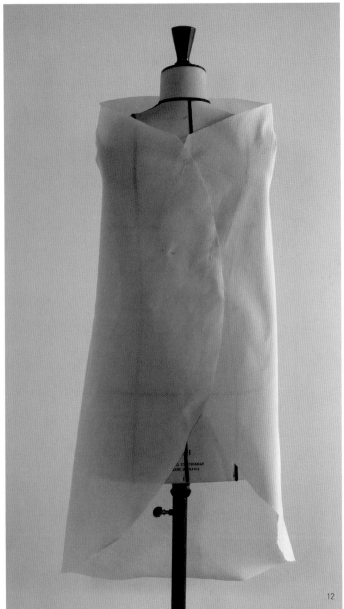

11. To assemble the dress, place the first pattern piece on the mannequin, with the opening towards the back.

12. To close the piece, cross the fabric at the back and adjust it to match the measurements for the size that is being made, in this case size 8, then add the buttons.

13. Next, place the second circle on the mannequin. This time, the edges face the front and the armholes match those on the inner piece.

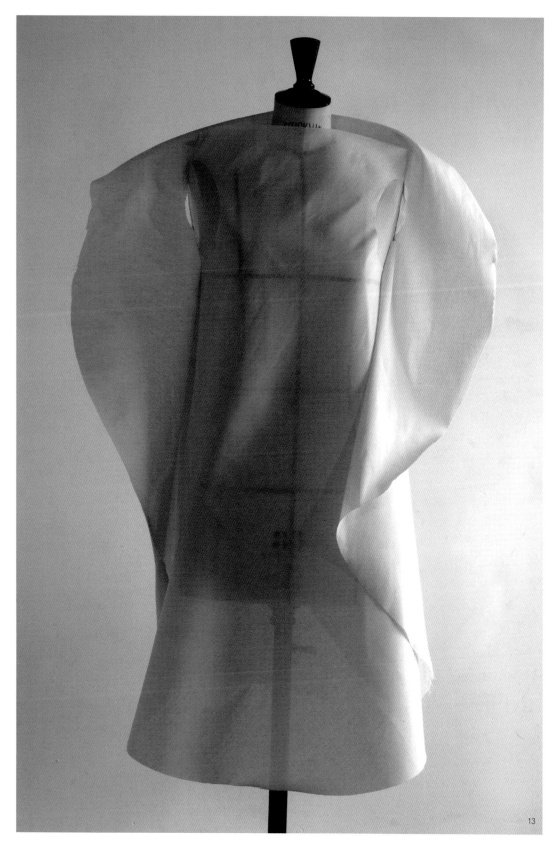

13

14

14. At the nape of the neck, fold the pattern piece back to shape a generous collar that almost reaches the shoulder.

15. Cross the piece in front and place eyelets at chest height where the ties will go. Having only one closing point will give a slight flare to the dress shape.

15

SQUARE:
ADJUSTABLE DRESS

This dress with a halter neck has a hook and eye on the front train that allows it to be worn two ways: one version has the natural hang of an evening gown; for the second version, you can hook the train on the loop at the back and drape it over either hip for the length of a cocktail dress.

In addition to offering dual possibilities in length, the dress can be gathered to the right or to the left using the fabric as an accessory.

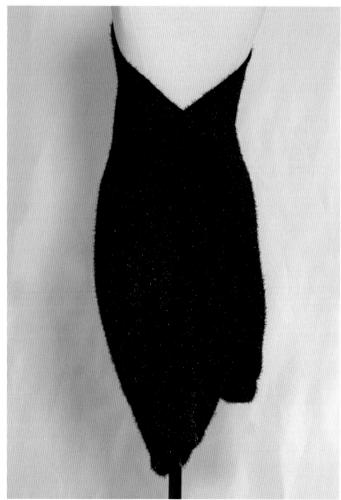

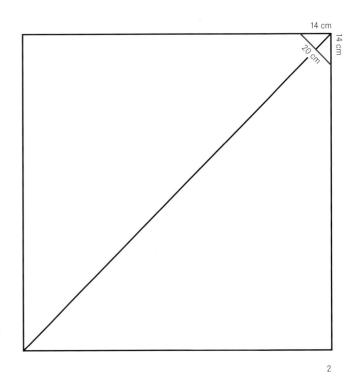

1. The base for this pattern is the square, a geometric figure with four equal sides and four right angles. The first step is to draw a square with 140 cm sides.

2. Draw a diagonal line as shown. In the top right corner of the square, draw a right-angled triangle where each side measures 14 cm and the base is 20 cm. Use this base as the line for cutting the pattern.

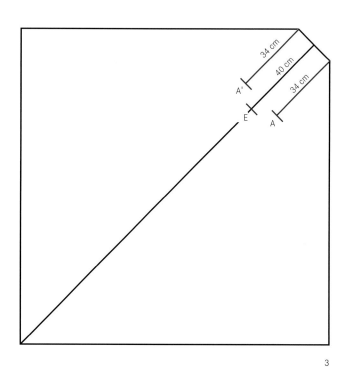

3

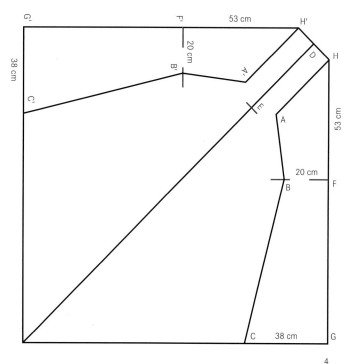

4

3. On the main diagonal line, measure 40 cm down to point E. From the top right corners, draw two 34 cm parallel lines on either side of the diagonal as shown in figure 3.

4. From point H, measure down 53 cm to point F. Draw a 20 cm perpendicular line from F to the left to point B. From point G at the bottom right corner, measure 38 cm to the left to point C. Join points C, B, A and H. Repeat this step with the same measurements using H' and G' as points of reference to mark points F', B' and C'. Join points C', B', A' and H'.

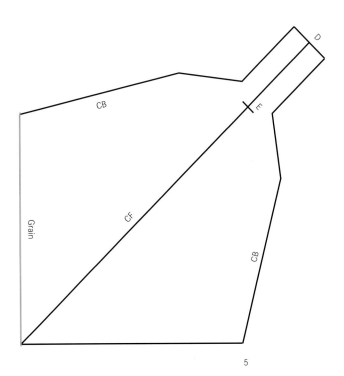

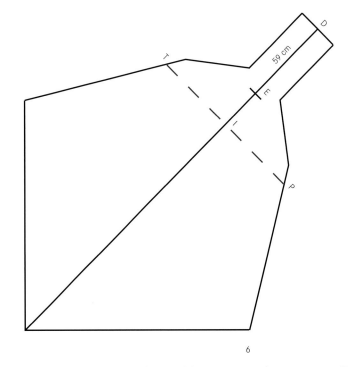

5. Cut this new pattern once from the fabric then open it along line D--E, which is the front neckline.

6. From point D on the diagonal line, measure 59 cm to point I. From here, draw a perpendicular line to both sides of the pattern ending at points T and P.

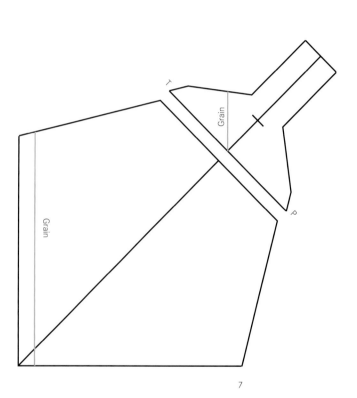

7

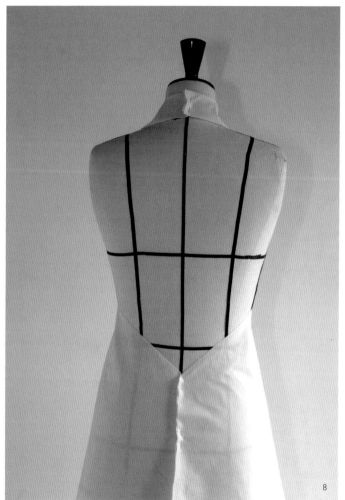

8

7. Cut the pattern along line T–P. Cut the resulting pattern piece for the upper part once with the fabric and once with the interfacing. Cut the pattern for the lower part once using the lining.

8. Place the dress on the mannequin with the opening to the back, and join the edges at the center back.

9. Sew the entire center back seam to completely close the dress skirt.

10. Adjust the neck to fit and measure for a buckle, or hook and eye, to open and close the upper part of the dress.

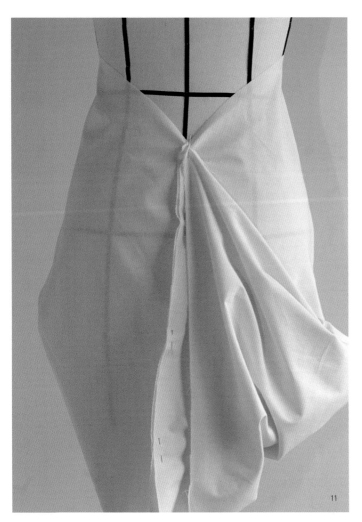

11. Take the center of the triangle of fabric at the front of the dress and wrap it around one side to the back neckline.

12. To gather and droop the volume that is created, depending on the occasion, place a small hook at the corner of the center front and a small loop of thread at the base of the center back neckline.

SQUARE AND RECTANGLE: SCARF BACK DRESS

The upper front on this design has a fitted V-neckline, thanks to the dart in the center chest. At the hip, the skirt volume is shaped to look like a dress with enormous pockets while the back looks like a large draped scarf.

The uniqueness of this dress is that it combines different styles in the front and back. While the front plays with geometric lines, the back emphasizes its loose, fluid hang.

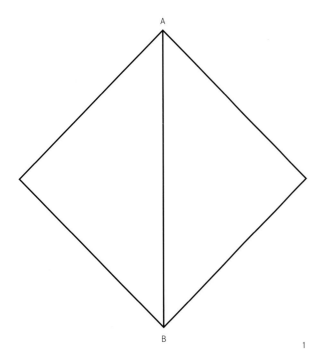

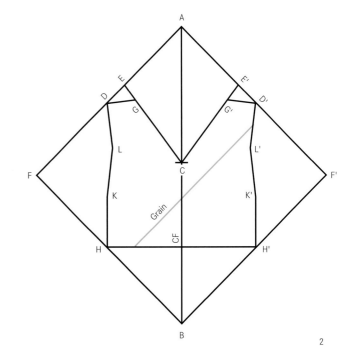

1. For this dress, make one pattern piece from a square and one from a rectangle. To start, draw a 56 x 56 cm square then draw a diagonal from A to B.

2. For the front piece, measure 36 cm from point A to point C at the center. Also from point A, measure 29 cm along the left side to point D, and along the same line, measure 22 cm from point A to point E. Repeat on right side for points E' (22 cm) and D' (29 cm). From point E, measure 5 cm down the E–C line to make point G then join G and D. Repeat on opposite side for point G', connecting it to D'.

From point B at the bottom of the diagonal line, measure 29 cm along the left side to make point H, and along the right side for point H'. Connect point H and H'. From point H, draw a 13.5 cm line, at a right angle to H–H', to make point K that is parallel to the diagonal line (A–B). Repeat for H' to create point K'.

From point D, draw a 12 cm line to make point L at a right angle to D–G. Now join L and K. Repeat this step for the opposite side to make point L', and connect it to point K'.

Cut the pattern along the line connecting these points: H'-K'-L'-D'-G'-C-G-D-L-K-H-H'.

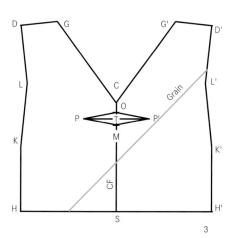

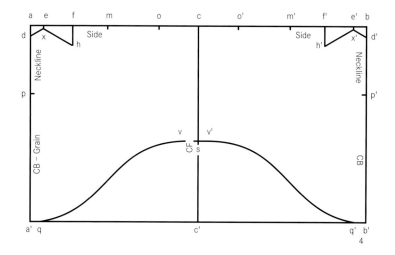

3. From point C, on line C–S, measure 2 cm down to point O then 1.5 cm down to point T and another 1.5 cm down to point M, so that the distance from C to M is 5 cm. On either side of point T, measure 7 cm to points P and P'. Now, join these four points O-P'-M-P to make the chest dart. Cut this pattern piece once with the fabric and once with the lining.

4. For the back and the skirt pattern piece, draw a 170 cm × 96 cm rectangle and mark the points c and c' in the middle of the long sides. From point a at the top left corner, measure 6.5 cm down to point d and 5.5 cm to the right to point e. From point e, draw a 1.5 cm perpendicular line down to point x. Join x and d. Return to point a and measure 21 cm to the right to point f then measure down 10 cm at a right angle to make point h. Join h and x. From point d, measure 32 cm down to point p and place a notch here; the line d–p is the back neckline.

From f, measure 20 cm to the right to point m and place a notch here. From point c, measure 20 cm to the left to point o and place another notch here. From point c, measure down 56 cm to point s on the center line. To the left of point s, draw a 5 cm perpendicular line to point v. From point a' at the bottom left corner, measure 5 cm to the right to point q. Join q and v with a curved line. Repeat the above with the same measurements for points d', e', x', f', h', p', m', o', v' and q'. Cut the pattern along the line connecting d-x-h-f-f'-h'-x'-d'-b'-q'-v'-v-q-a'-d; mark the pattern piece once on the fabric and once on the lining.

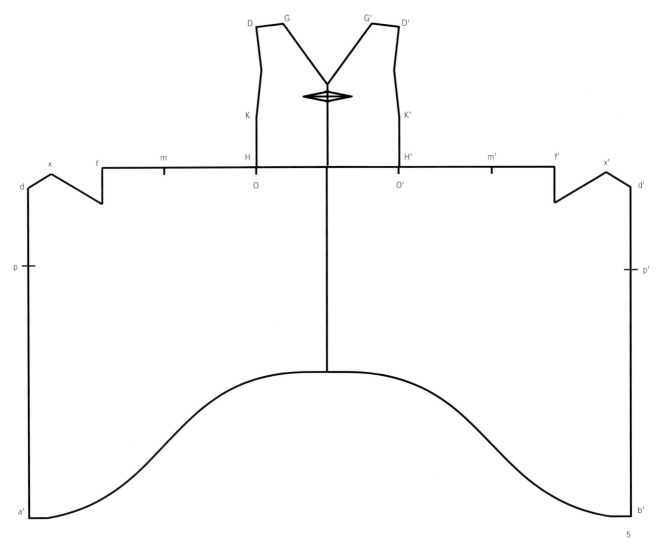

5

5. To assemble the dress, place the pattern pieces as shown in figure 5. First, close the waist by joining H–H' to o–o'. Make sure that the center fronts line up with each other. Next, sew the shoulders joining D–G to d–x and G'–D' to x'–d'. Close the center back joining p'–b' to p–a'. Join m to o, and m' to o' and sew the notches between these points. Join the sides K–H to f–m, and K'–H' to m'–f'.

6. This photograph shows the dress during assembly when the skirt volume is in the shape of an irregular triangle.

6

7. Now, adjust the volume of the skirt. To do so, take the peak of the excess fabric that resulted on the left side when m and o were joined. Fold it towards the inside of the dress as shown in the figures 7 and 8. Do the same with the peak on the right side.

8. This photograph shows the dress's final silhouette where the folds look like enormous pockets.

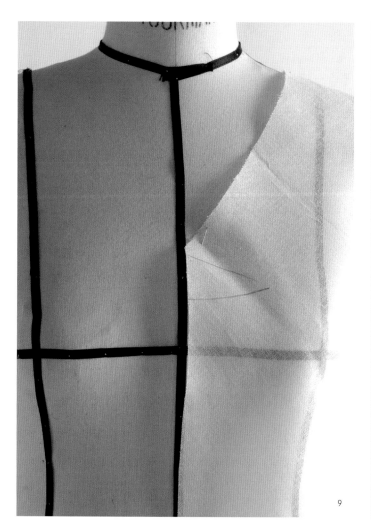

9

10

9. Once you have the desired silhouette, close the chest dart.

10. When this dress is sewn, remember to retain its oval shape.

RECTANGLE:
WRAP AROUND DRESS

This dress uses the sarong style, which is normally used for informal dresses. However, in this case the dress is made with paillettes, a sequined fabric that immediately turns it into an evening dress. This dress has a pronounced neckline at the back. Tie the dress at the neck with delicate drawstrings.

To give weight to the ends of the drawstrings, hang ceramic balls or beads that match the chosen fabric. In this case semitransparent pebbles are used that match the shimmering fabric.

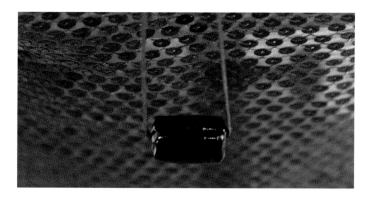

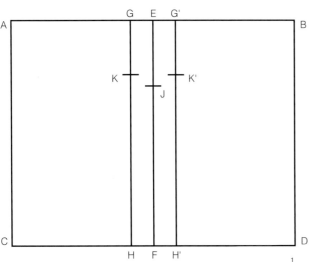

1. Draw a 130 cm x 100 cm rectangle with corner points A–B–D–C. Divide it in half with line E–F. From point E measure 10 cm to the right to make point G' and 10 cm to the left to mark point G. Draw lines from points G' and G, parallel to line E–F that end at H' and H on line C–D. From center point E, measure 29 cm down to make point J; from point G, measure 24 cm down to make K; and from point G', measure 24 cm down to make K'. Make buttonholes at points K, J and K'. Cut this pattern piece once using the sequined fabric.

2. To assemble the dress, hang the pattern on the mannequin placing line E–F along the center back. Cross the fabric rectangle in front as shown in the photograph.

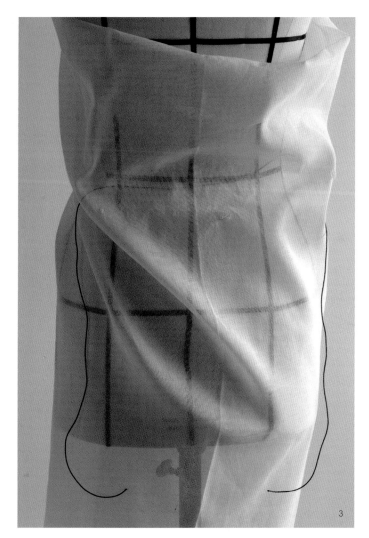

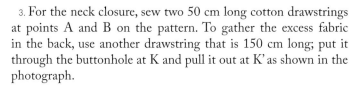

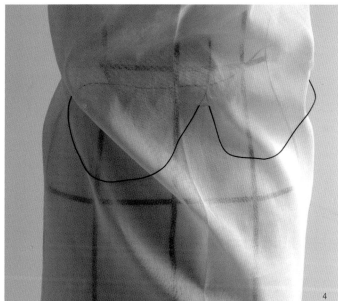

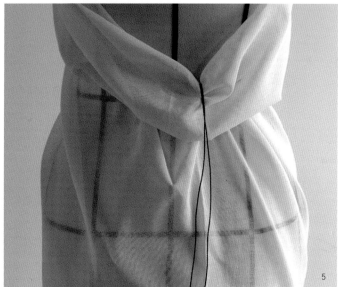

3. For the neck closure, sew two 50 cm long cotton drawstrings at points A and B on the pattern. To gather the excess fabric in the back, use another drawstring that is 150 cm long; put it through the buttonhole at K and pull it out at K' as shown in the photograph.

4-5. Now, pass both ends of the drawstring through J and gather the fabric. Knot the ends of the drawstring and hang a bead there.

RECTANGLE:
LACE DRESS WITH BATWING SLEEVE

The body for this dress reminds us of the kimono's detached silhouette. The traditional Japanese kimono also has extremely wide, large loose sleeves. However, unlike the kimono, which is open and fitted with a wide sash, this dress is closed and has a zipper.

Lace is a very delicate fabric that was created in the 16th century. Since then it has not gone out of fashion. Sewing machines have a special foot for sewing lace, which needs a 1.5 mm to 3 mm stitch.

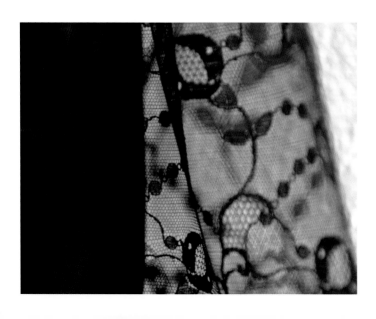

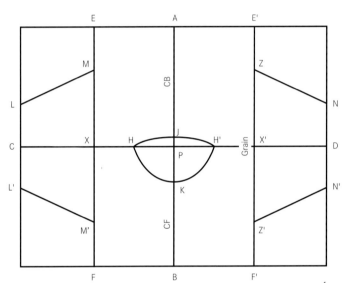

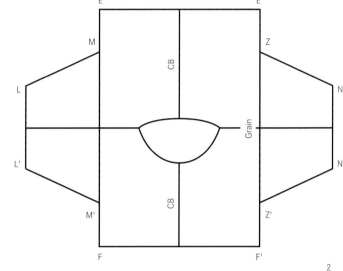

1. For this dress, draw a 90 cm x 68 cm rectangle then divide it into four quadrants by drawing lines A–B and C–D that intersect at point P. From point P, measure: 12 cm to the left and to the right for points H and H', respectively; 3 cm up to point J; and 10 cm down to point K. Join points H–J–H'–K for the neckline. From point A, measure 22 cm to the left for point E and to the right for point E'. Draw a line from point E down to F, parallel to line A-B. Repeat for E' to create point F". Line E–F intersects line C–D at point X; line E'–F' intersects line C–D at point X'. From point X, measure 22 cm up to point M and 22 cm down to point M'; from point X', measure 22 cm up to point Z and 22 cm down to point Z'. From point C, measure 12 cm up to point L and 12 cm down to point L'; join L to M, and L' to M'. From point D, measure 12 cm up to point N and 12 cm down to point N'; join N to Z, and N' to Z'.

2. Cut the pattern along the line E'-Z-N-N'-Z'-F'-F-M'-L'-L-M-E-E', then mark it and cut it once with the velvet and once with the lining. To assemble the dress, close the sleeves by joining L–M with L'–M' on the left side and Z–N with Z'–N' on the right. To sew the sides, join E–M with M'–F on the left side and E'–Z' with Z'–F' on the right.

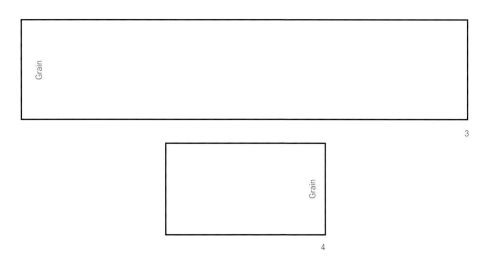

Grain

Grain

3

4

3-4. For the overskirt, draw a 280 cm × 61 cm rectangle as in figure 3; cut it once in lace. For the skirt, draw a 100 cm × 56 cm rectangle as in figure 4; cut it once in crepe.

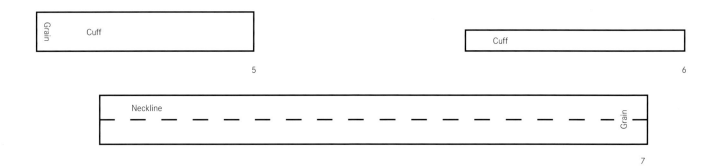

Grain Cuff

5

Cuff

6

Neckline Grain

7

5. There are two layers of cuffs on this dress: the upper cuff is a bit shorter than the inner cuff. For the inner cuff, draw a 50 cm x 9 cm rectangle and cut it twice using stretch tulle.

6. For the shorter upper cuff, draw a 50 cm x 5 cm rectangle and cut it twice using stretch tulle.

7. For the neckline, draw a 250 cm x 22 cm neckline and cut it once using stiff tulle.

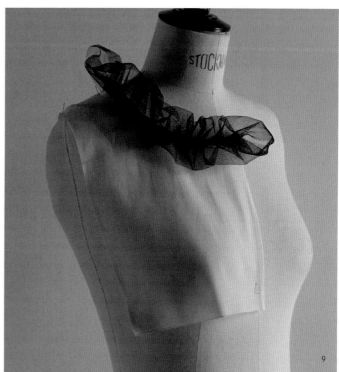

8. Place the bodice pattern on the mannequin and close it. Pucker the recently made tulle neckline piece but do not worry too much about making uniform ruffles. Sew the tulle to the dress neckline, which will curl slightly.

9. Now fold the tulle piece in half and curl each ruffle separately for more volume. To finish assembling this dress, sew the lightly puckered cuffs, the skirt and the overskirt.

RECTANGLE:
SCARF DRESS

This dress is cut on the bias and has a lot of movement. It is fitted at the shoulders and the chest then loosens as it hangs down. Given the cut of the neckline, the shape of the armholes and the different levels of the hem, it is surprising that the entire dress is made from one rectangle with an opening.

This dress is an example of how a simple pattern can result in an elaborate dress and how attractive proportions can be achieved with seams.

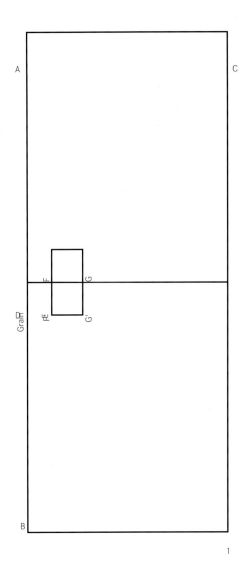

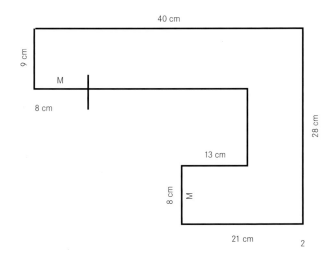

1. Draw a 180 cm × 75 cm rectangle with D as the midpoint along line A–B. From point D, measure 9 cm at a right angle from A-B toward the center of the fabric to point E. Above and below point E, measure 12 cm to points F and F', F-F' should be parallel to A-B. Create a rectangle by measuring 12 cm to the right of points F and F' to points G and G', respectively. This should create a 24 cm x 12 cm rectangle. Cut this pattern twice in the crepe fabric.

2. This pattern is the dress collar facing. Draw the pattern by following the measurements on figure 2. Keep in mind that all of the corners are right angles. Cut the pattern twice in the chosen fabric and twice in the interfacing. Before assembling the dress, finish the two rectangles by machine with a border of at least 0.5 cm.

3. To assemble the dress, place the two rectangles on the mannequin and match line D–E to the shoulder and the armhole. Join both pieces at the front and back. Decide on the length of the necklines and mark them with a pin. Sew the pieces from this point downward but without too much pressure since they are on the bias.

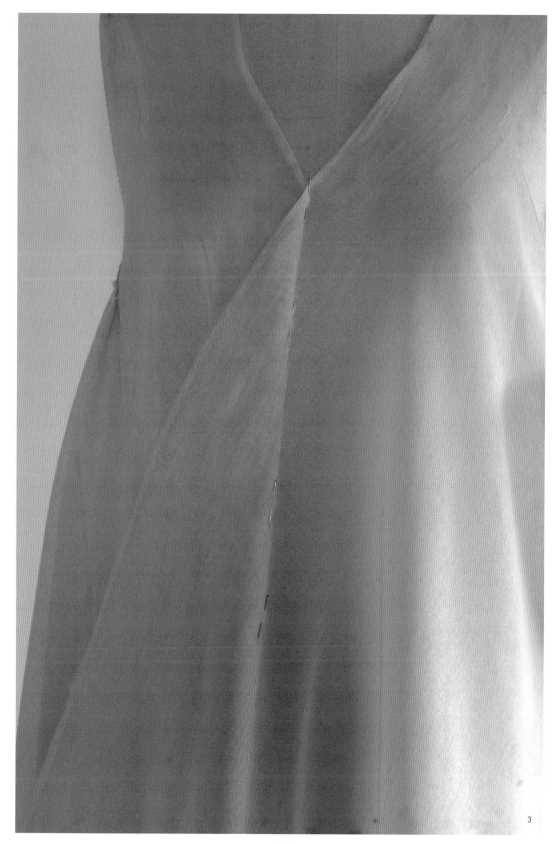

3

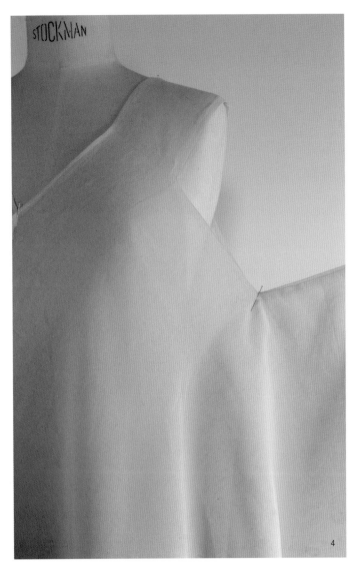

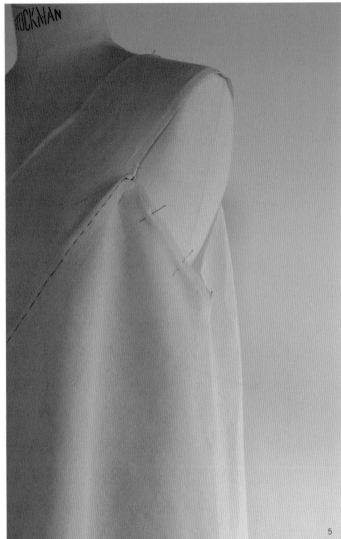

4. Now, join the armholes with a pin and find the desired width, as shown in figure 4.

5. Move the excess fabric in the armhole forward on the left side and to the back on the right side then sew the armhole. This balances the volume of the dress.

DRESS WITH ASYMMETRICAL HEMLINE

This dress bodice is inspired by the famous dress worn by Audrey Hepburn in *Breakfast at Tiffany's,* now known as the best dress in film history. By contrast, the draping of this skirt is much more modern and comes from a circle and a square. The combination of the bodice and this skirt results in a totally chic garment.

The cut of the dress has a high waist. The bodice is tailored by two darts in the shape of a cross in the center front and center chest, as shown in the photograph.

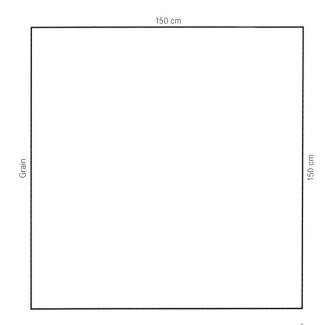

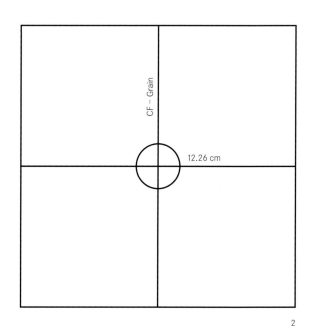

1. Start the pattern for this asymmetrical dress by drawing a square with sides that measure 150 cm.

2. Mark the center points for each side and join them with two perpendicular lines. Where the lines intersect at the center of the square, make a circle with a 12.26 cm radius. Cut this pattern once in velvet.

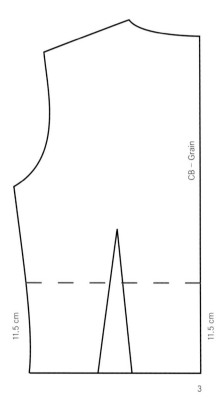

CB – Grain

11.5 cm

11.5 cm

3

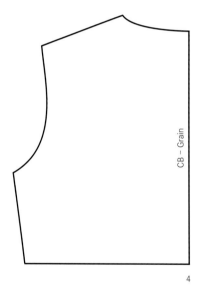

CB – Grain

4

3. Now, take the basic back pattern (page 59) and shorten the bottom by 11.5 cm using a straight line.

4. Cut the pattern along the line you just drew, ignoring the dart that was there.

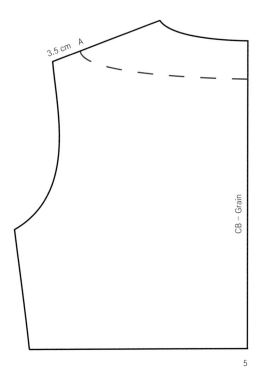

3.5 cm A

CB – Grain

5

CB – Grain

6

5. To create the neckline, adjust the width of the shoulder by measuring 3.5 cm from the edge of the armhole to point A. From point A, draw a straight line to the center back with just a hint of a curve at the shoulder.

6. Cut the altered back pattern piece twice in velvet and twice in the lining.

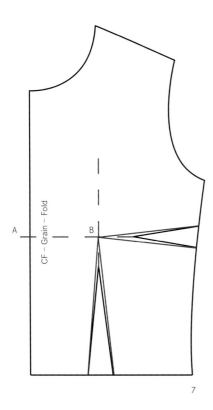

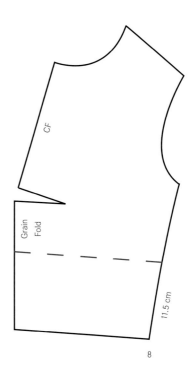

7. Now, take a basic front pattern. Extend the two darts, lengthening both until they intersect at point B. Close the darts and open the pattern along line A–B.

8. Shorten the front bodice by 11.5 cm but do not use a straight line; instead follow the curve of line A–B.

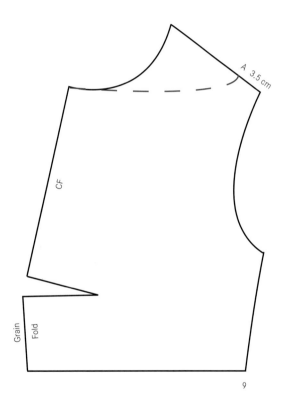

9

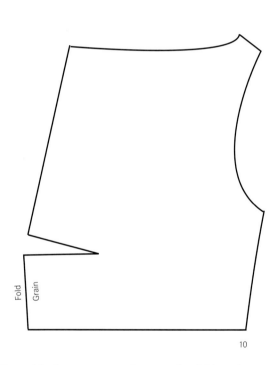

10

9. As in the back piece, reduce the width of the shoulder to 3.5 cm. Draw a line from point A to the corner of the center front. For the neckline, use a straight line but leave a small curve at the beginning of the shoulder.

10. Place this front pattern piece on the fold, and cut once in velvet and once in lining.

11. To assemble the pattern pieces, first place the front and back patterns on the mannequin and join them together. Close the darts as shown in figure 11. Sew the skirt to the bodice.

11

DRESS WITH HIGH WAIST

This dress has a tight bodice and is tailored at the waist. The full skirt combines color and texture, as it is made from three circles in different fabrics: smooth taffeta, printed taffeta and printed silk organza. The skirt includes a quarter circle made out of the banana fiber *sinamay*, which is thicker than the other three fabrics and is rigid enough to support them.

For weight, beads are hung on the two chains that are used as dress straps. Both chains are joined at the front neckline with a single jet stone, imitating a necklace, and at the back a pebble hangs from each drawstring.

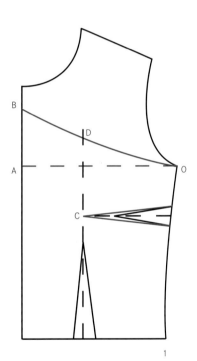

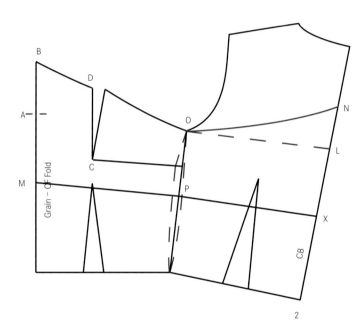

1. Start with the basic front pattern (page 59). From point O, draw a perpendicular line to the opposite edge of the pattern that intersects the center front to make point A. From point A, measure 8 cm up to point B. Use a curved line to join point B to point O. Extend the center of the waist dart to cross line B–O, making point D; extend the chest dart to meet the waist dart extension, making point C. Close the chest dart and open a new dart on line D–C. Cut the top of the pattern along line B–O.

2. Join the sides of this pattern and a basic back pattern. From point O, measure 10 cm down to point P; from point A, measure 10.5 cm down to make point M. Use a straight line to join points M and P. From point O, draw a perpendicular line to the right edge of the pattern that intersects the center back to make point L. From point L, measure up 6.5 cm to point N. Use a lightly curved line to join N to O. Finally, from point L measure 10.5 cm down to point X. Join X to P on the side seam. Cut the pattern along the lines M–P–X and B–O–N.

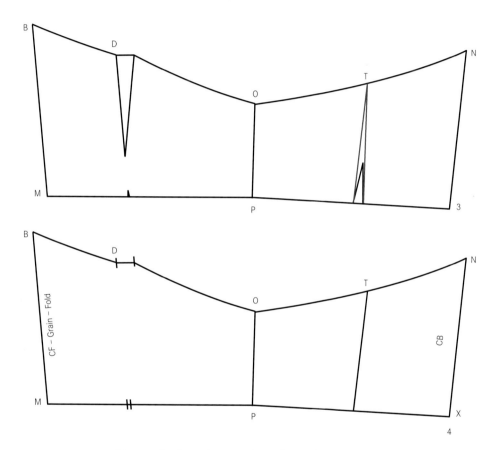

3-4. Change the front darts to pleats. Extend the waist dart on the back to point T on the opposite edge of the pattern then close the dart. The resulting pattern seen in figure 4 is cut on the fold once in the shiny taffeta and once in the lining.

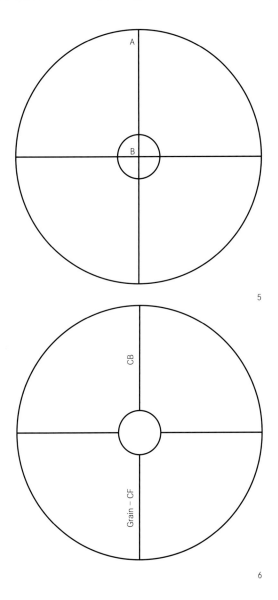

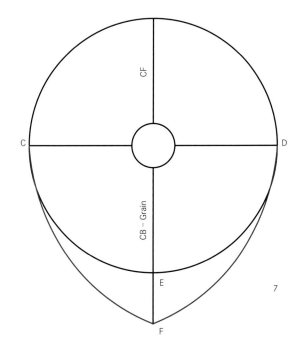

5. Now, draw a circle with a 75 cm radius, which is the distance from point A to point B. From the same center point B, draw another circle with a 13.3 cm radius.

6. Cut this pattern once in the plain black taffeta, once in the striped black taffeta and once in the checkered silk organza.

7. For the final pattern piece, extend the vertical diameter of the larger circle. To do this, from point E measure 30 cm down to point F. Join points C, F and D with a curved line. Cut this pattern once in black *sinamay*.

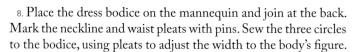

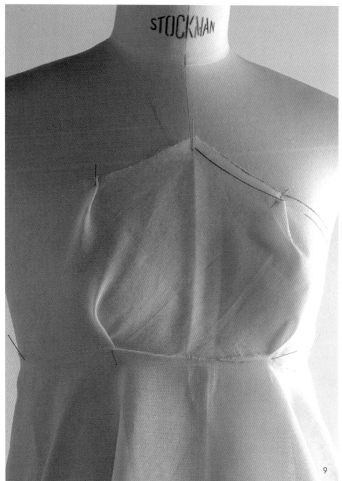

8. Place the dress bodice on the mannequin and join at the back. Mark the neckline and waist pleats with pins. Sew the three circles to the bodice, using pleats to adjust the width to the body's figure.

9. Once the pieces are joined, adjust the chest pleats to perfection since they are fundamental to the silhouette and the fit of this dress. Now, place the elongated *sinamay* circle on the mannequin with the tip, point F, at the back and gather it to point N on the bodice pattern. To finish, sew two delicate chains from point B on the front neckline to point N on the back to use as straps for the dress.

DRESS WITH A TUXEDO COLLAR

This type of collar belongs on formal attire, which explains the use of velvet and lace here. A golden fabric is used underneath the skirt, highlighting the motifs. If something more discreet is preferred, use black fabric so that only one texture is noticed. On the other hand, if something more daring is preferred, use bright colors like fuchsia and lemon green.

Use an invisible zipper to close the dress. The advantage is that when the zipper is closed it looks like a seam. Place the zipper on the center back or the left side seam, wherever it is more comfortable.

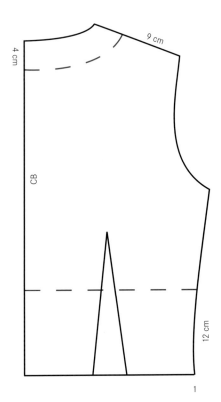

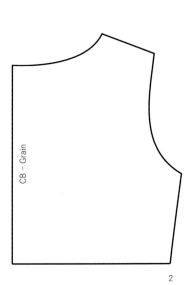

1. Use the basic back pattern (page 59) but alter it so that the neckline is 4 cm lower than the original and the shoulder measurement is reduced to 9 cm. Also, raise the hem by 12 cm.

2. Cut the resulting pattern twice in the selected velvet fabric and twice in the lining.

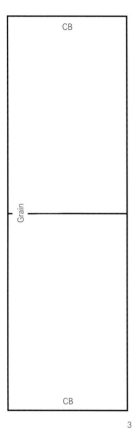

CB

Grain

CB

3

Grain

CB

CF

CB

4

3. For the skirt, draw a 75 cm × 240 cm rectangle and divide it in half horizontally. Cut the pattern once using the golden or colored fabric that goes underneath and once in the lining.

4. For the overskirt, draw a 150 cm × 75 cm rectangle and divide it in half vertically along the center front. Cut this pattern once using the lace fabric.

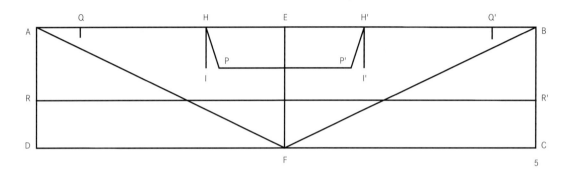

5. For the front, draw a 114 cm × 27 cm rectangle with the points A–B–C–D as the corners and divide it in half vertically along line E–F. From point E, measure 18 cm to the left for point H, and to the right for point H'. At right angles to points H and H', measure 9 cm down to points I and I' respectively. From point I, measure 3 cm to the right to point P then join P to H. From point I', measure 3 cm to the left to point P' then join P' to H'. Join points P and P'. From point A, measure 10 cm to the right for point Q, and from B measure 10 cm to the left for point Q', then place a notch at both. From line D–C, measure up 10.5 cm to make line R–R'.

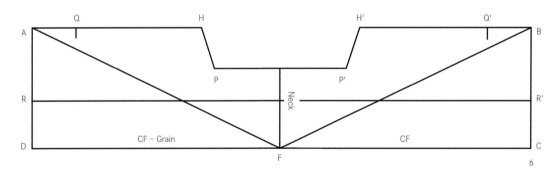

6. Cut this pattern once in the velvet fabric and once in the lining. The next step is to sew wire to this piece along the horizontal lines A-H, H'-Q', P–P', R-R' and D–C as well as the diagonals A–F and F–B.

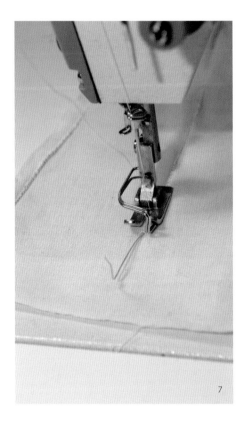

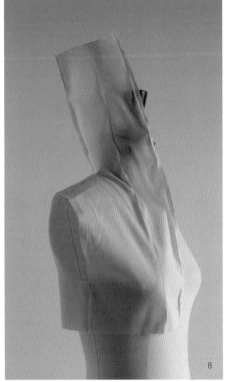

7. Carefully sew a thin rustproof wire to the front piece. Make sure the wire will not corrode when the garment is washed. Sew the wire by hand or by machine with a small zigzag stitch.

8. Assemble this pattern on the mannequin. Keep in mind that the armholes are lines Q–H and H'–Q', the shoulders are lines H–P and P'–H' and the neck is line P–P'. Join the front and the back pattern pieces.

9. Shape the collar and neckline by folding the wires to achieve the desired volume and appearance. Now that the bodice is finished, sew the pieces for the skirt and overskirt.

TUBE TOP DRESS

To make a strapless or tube top dress, use a stretchy fabric that hugs the body and gives a person freedom of movement, making the dress more comfortable. For this design the creator of the dress, Miguel Madriz, chose stretch satin and combined it with tulle on the skirt.

The satin bows are decorative rather than functioning elements so they can be accentuated. Here, the front bow is in the color fuchsia and the back bow is much longer than the dress.

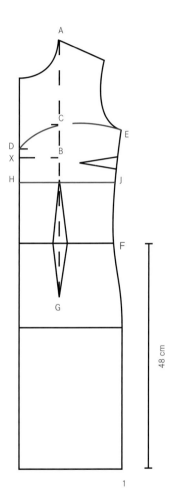

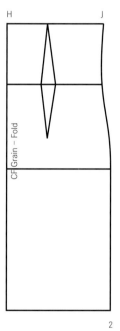

1. Cut the basic long front pattern with a 48 cm long skirt. Draw the line A–G. From point A, measure down 18 cm to point C and 25 cm to point B. At a right angle to B, mark point X on the center front. From point X, measure up 2 cm to point D. Use a curved line to join points D, C and E. Finally, from point F measure 13 cm up to J. At a right angle to J, mark point H on the center front.

2. The lower pattern piece below line H–J is cut on the fold, once in stretch satin and once in lining. Use a knit lining for this dress.

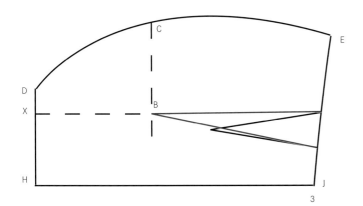

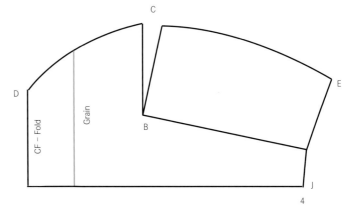

3. The upper pattern piece above line H–J is cut along line D–C–E. Extend the chest dart to point B then close it and open a new one along line C–B.

4. Cut the pattern piece for the upper part of the dress on the fold, once in stretch satin and once in the knit lining.

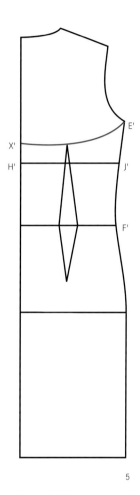

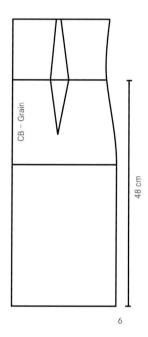

5

6

5. Now take the basic long back pattern with the same 48 cm long skirt as in the base model. From point F', measure 13 cm up to point J'. At a right angle to J', mark point H' on the center back. From point H', measure 4 cm up to point X'. Join points X' and E' with a curved line that crosses the tip of the dart.

6. The lower part of the pattern is cut twice in stretch satin and twice in knit lining.

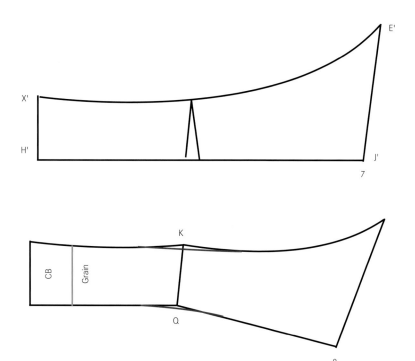

7-8. On the upper pattern piece, close the dart and smooth out points K and Q as in figure 8. Cut this pattern piece twice in stretch satin and twice in knit lining.

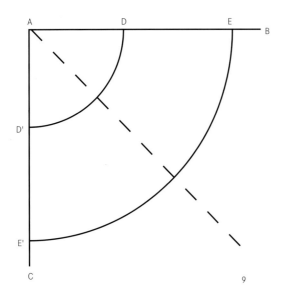

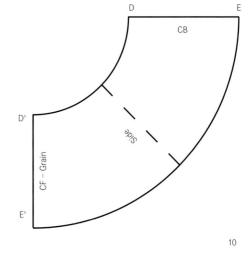

9. For the dress ruffle, draw a right angle with points C, A and B. From center point A, draw one quarter of a circle with a 26.2 cm radius to points D and D', and another with a 56.2 cm radius to points E and E'.

10. Cut the pattern along D–E–E'–D'–D and cut it twice in stretch satin and twice in the knit lining.

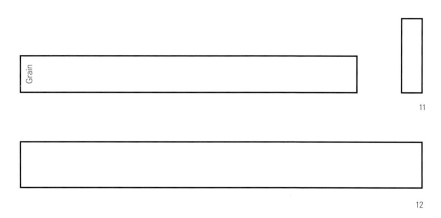

Grain

11

12

11. For the front bow, draw a 46 cm × 5 cm rectangle and cut it twice in the fuchsia satin. Now draw a 10 cm × 3 cm rectangle and cut it once in the fuchsia satin.

12. For the back bow, draw and cut two 220 cm × 25 cm rectangles in black silk satin.

13

13. Finally, for the overskirt, draw and cut two 100 cm × 200 cm rectangles in black tulle.

14. To assemble the dress, place on the mannequin the four pieces for the dress: front bodice, back bodice, front skirt and back skirt. Now sew the ruffle at the same height as the skirt.

15. For the last step gather the ruffle a bit to give it volume as shown in the photograph and assemble the tulle rectangles in two layers so they bulge over top of the skirt. To finish, place the fuchsia bow on the chest and the black bow at the back.

DRESS WITH CAMELLIA SKIRT

This dress is classic and elegant with a silhouette that evokes Christian Dior's "New Look" from the glamorous 1950s. It is cut at the waist and has a tight bodice with armhole darts. The top contrasts with the ample skirt volume that is created with three circles of fabric. To accentuate the silhouette, a rigid fabric is used that does not drape very much.

The hem of the dress is adorned with camellias, a flower with large pronounced petals. Though the camellia is usually used in wedding dresses, this example shows that it is the perfect adornment for a sensible cocktail dress.

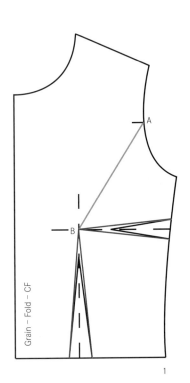

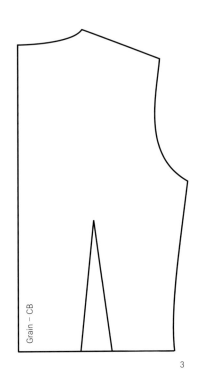

1. Take the basic front pattern and extend the tips of the darts until they intersect at point B. From point B, draw a line to point A in the middle of the armhole and close the darts.

2. Cut this pattern on the fold, once in the fabric chosen for the dress and once in lining.

3. For the back of the dress, use the basic back pattern and cut it twice in the fabric and twice in lining.

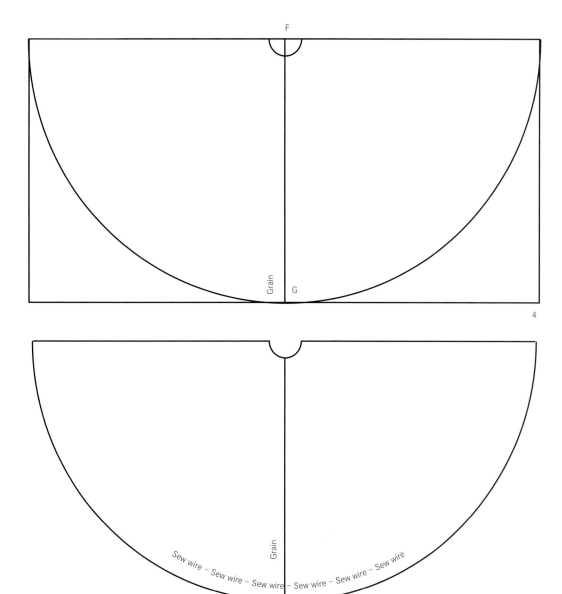

4. Now, draw a 110 cm × 55 cm rectangle and divide it in half vertically with line F–G. From the center point F, draw a semicircle with a 55 cm radius, which is the length of the skirt, and another smaller one with a 3.6 cm radius.

5. The resulting pattern is the skirt for the dress. Cut it six times in the fabric.

6. To assemble the dress, place the front and back pattern pieces on the mannequin, close the chest darts and sew the pieces together.

7. Now sew the skirt to the bodice. To do so, sew the semicircles to the front and back, and to each other.

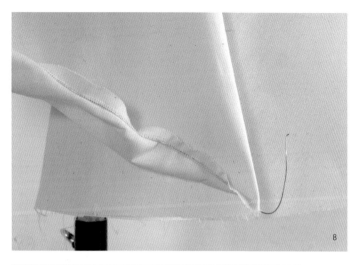

8-9. With a zigzag stitch, sew a wire 2 cm from the edge of the skirt hem. Use a rustproof wire that is easy to manipulate. The wire's thickness depends on the weight of the fabric; here, we recommend using a wire with medium thickness. Give the dress more volume by folding the hem into the shapes of camellias.

BASIC SKIRT PATTERN

SCALE 1:4

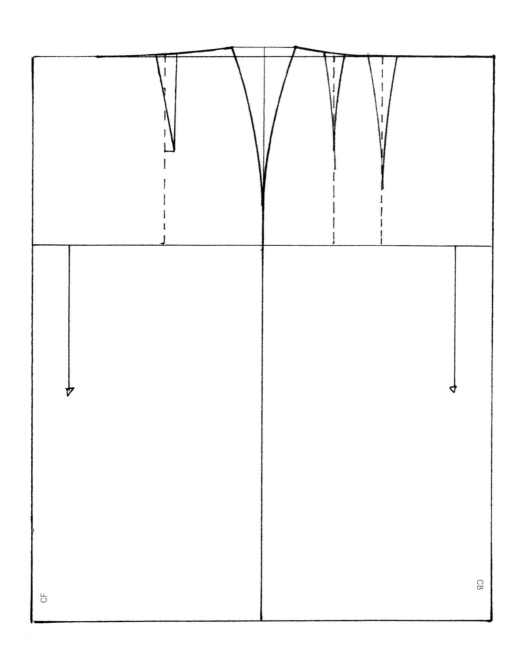

BASIC DRESS PATTERN

SCALE 1:4

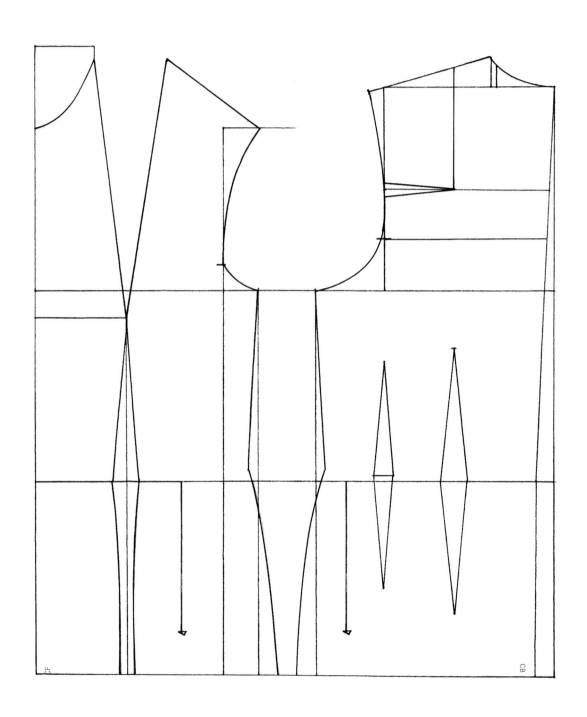

BASIC SLEEVE PATTERN

SCALE 1:4

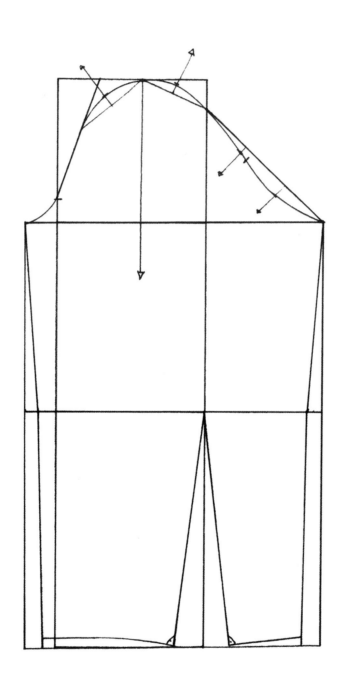

SINGLE-SEAM PATTERN
WITH RIBBON FRINGES

DRESS: SCALE 1:7

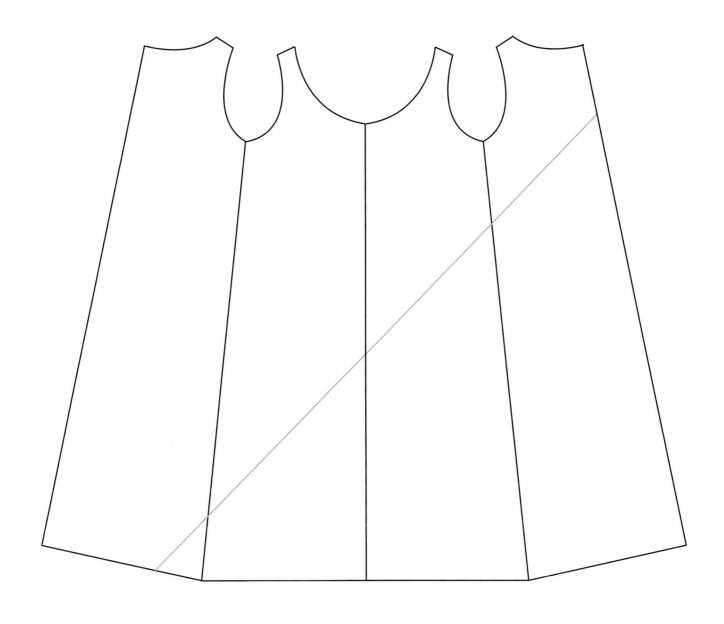

TIES: SCALE 1:2

SINGLE-SEAM PATTERN WITH TULLE RUFFLES

DRESS: SCALE 1:7

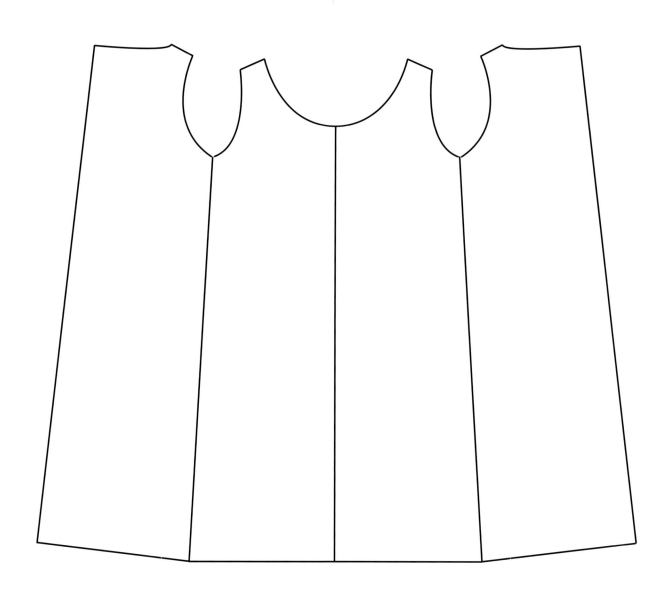

LINING: SCALE 1:7

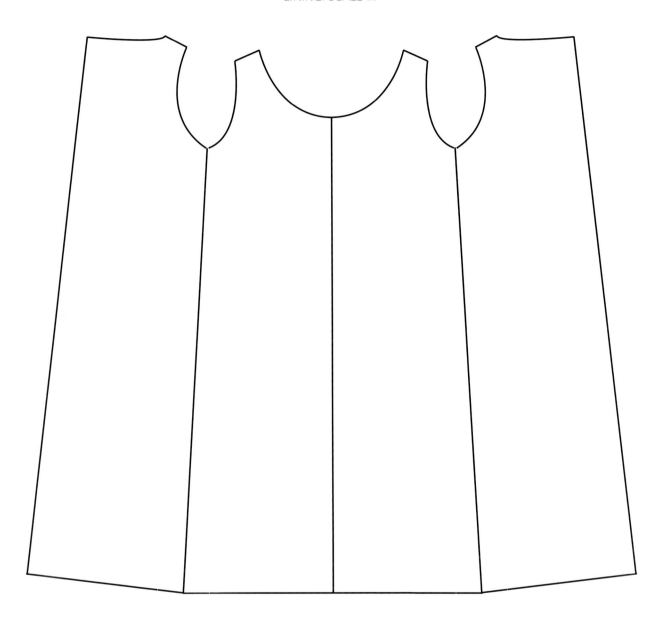

RUFFLES: SCALE 1:20

PATTERN FOR DRESS WITH BATWING SLEEVES

FRONT AND BACK: SCALE 1:4

SKIRT: SCALE 1:30

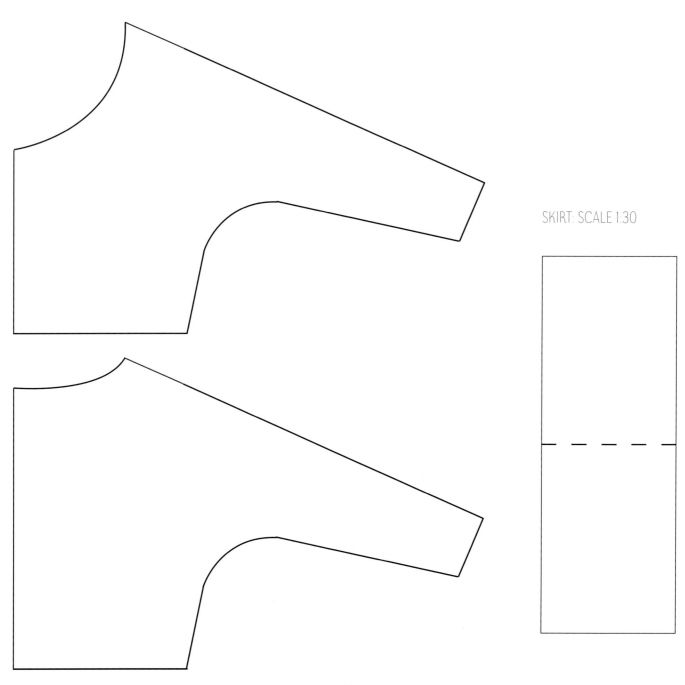

PATTERN FOR PLEATED DRESS

DRESS AND COLLAR: SCALE 1:7

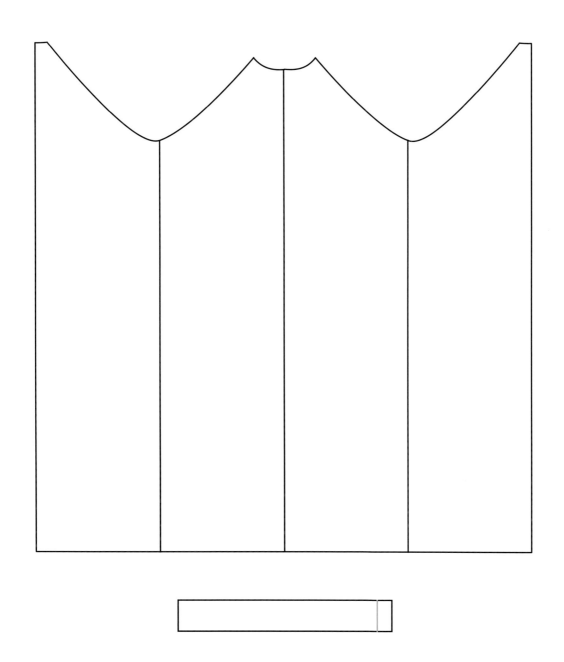

PATTERN FOR DRESS
WITH HALTER NECK

DRESS AND FACING: SCALE 1:10

PATTERN FOR COCOON SILHOUETTE DRESS

DRESS AND COLLAR FACING: SCALE 1:10

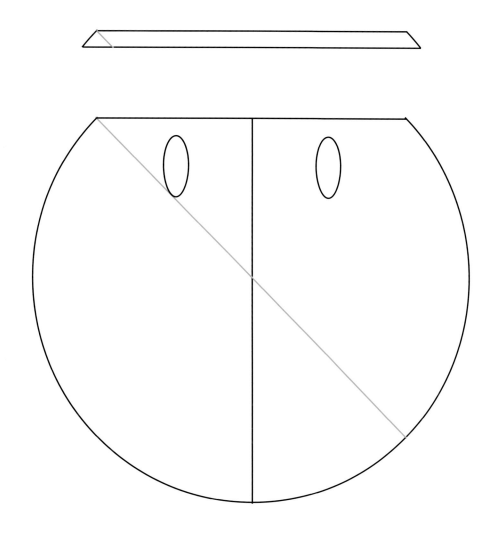

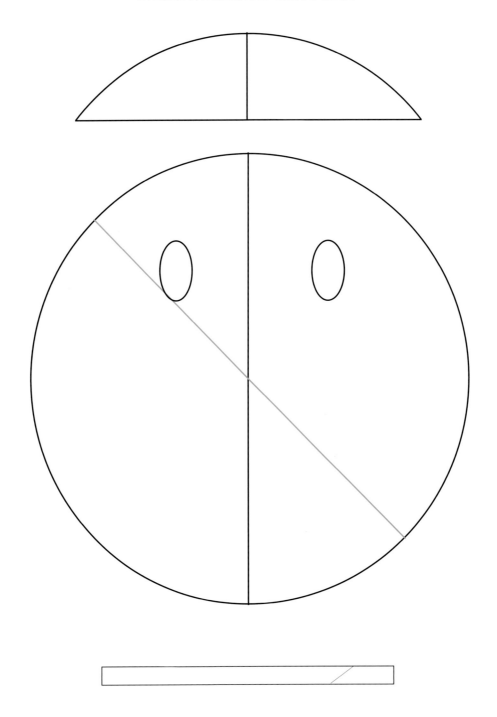

PATTERN FOR
SCARF BACK DRESS

FRONT PIECE AND DRESS: SCALE 1:10

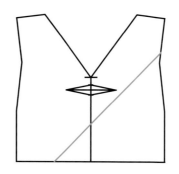

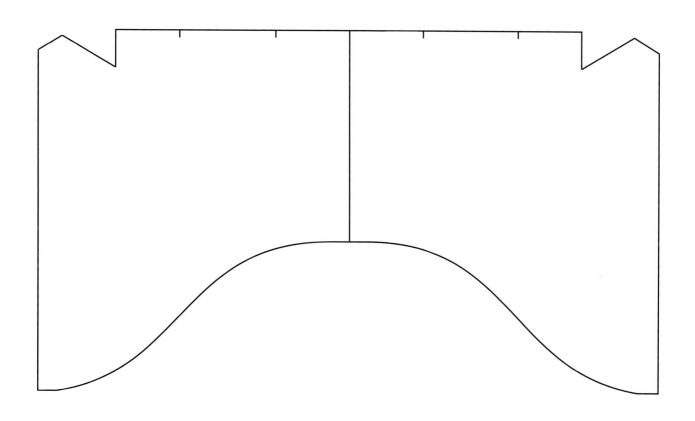

PATTERN FOR WRAP AROUND DRESS

SCALE 1:10

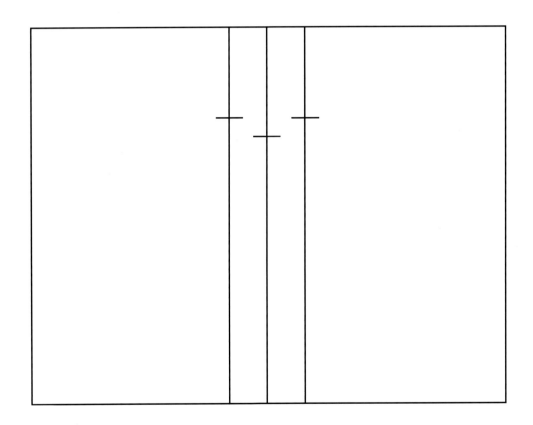

PATTERN FOR LACE DRESS
WITH BATWING SLEEVE

BODICE, CUFFS AND SKIRT: SCALE 1:10

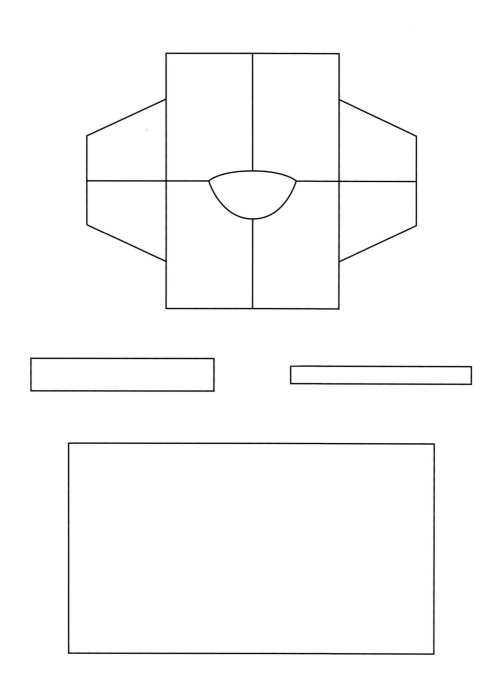

NECKLINE AND OVERSKIRT: SCALE 1:15

PATTERN FOR SCARF DRESS

FACING AND DRESS: SCALE 1:8

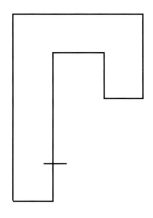

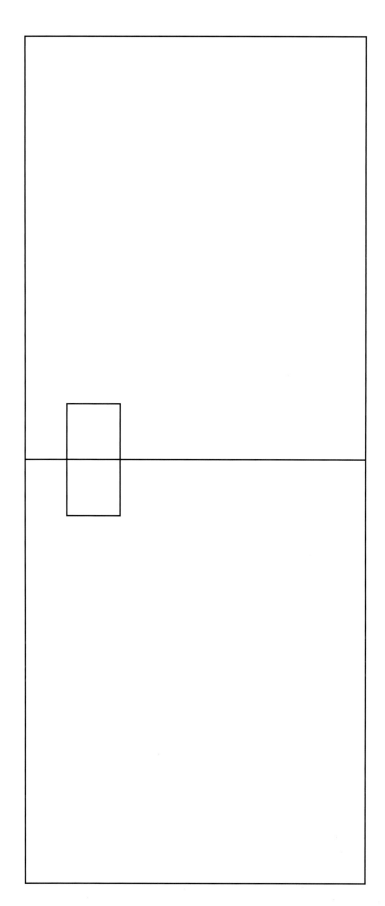

GLOSSARY OF PATTERN AND GARMENT MAKING TERMS

Against the grain: the horizontal direction of the fabric, or the weft.

Allowances: straight or round symbols at uneven edges created by altering the pattern.

Alter: to correct a pattern or part of it based on other measurements or shapes.

Appliqué: a pattern piece that is attached with thread to the cut pattern on the fabric.

Armhole: the hole in a garment that the arm passes through, or where the sleeve is sewn.

Assembly: the process of placing on a mannequin the different patterns that form a garment and joining them accordingly.

Back: the part of the dress or shirt that matches the back and covers it.

Backstitch: to sew straight stitches with a sewing machine.

Balloon: to embellish fabric with round folds.

Basque: the front bottom edge of a jacket or coat, located between the lowest button or the end of the zipper and the hem.

Bead: a pellet usually made from glass with a hole in the center for a cord or thread to pass through.

Bias: in a square of fabric, the bias is the line at a 45° angle that divides the square into two equal halves. Fabric that is cut on the bias is cut on a slant to the grain, which gives the garment movement and a softer drape with more fullness.

Buckle: an item in a variety of shapes that is used to adjust belts and straps. It is usually made out of metal or precious metals and has one or more central hinges.

Buttonhole: a hole with ribbed edges on the garment whose main function is to allow a button to pass through.

Casing: a fold made on a garment with room on the inside for a ribbon, elastic or drawstring to go through.

Center: axis or line that separates the right from the left side.

Center Back (CB): is an imaginary line in the back that divides the body in half vertically. In a pattern, the CB is the line that indicates where the center of the back of the body is.

Chest dart: this dart shapes the volume of the bust.

Center Front (CF): is an imaginary line in the front that divides the body in half vertically. In a pattern, the CF is the line that indicates where the center of the front of the body is.

Cocoon silhouette: a spacious garment silhouette that is achieved by ballooning the garment. In the 1920s Paul Poiret (1879–1944) was the first designer to use this silhouette, inspired by the silkworm cocoon. Since then, many designers have included it on runways around the world.

Collar: a strip of fabric that is attached to the upper part of some items of clothing and circles the neck.

Crimp: to make small folds either outwards or inwards on the fabric.

Cuff: the part of the garment sleeve that circles the wrist.

Cut piece: a piece that is marked on the pattern but attached to the fabric without thread.

Dart: a fold in an item of clothing that is sewn in the shape of a wedge or diamond in order to fit the fabric to the shape of the body. Sew the dart from the widest part to the narrowest part of the wedge, keeping it as flat as possible.

Drape: a basic characteristic of every fabric that depends on how it was manufactured and the weight of the fiber. Fabrics with the best drape are made from natural fibers.

Edges: the open ends that are folded inwards and sewn or stuck together to finish. They are usually the lower ends of the arm and entire garment. Edges are sewn in different ways depending on the type of fabric used.

Evasée: a garment's flared silhouette.

Even: to sew together two different lengths of fabric without folds emerging. For example, to sew a front shoulder seam to a back shoulder seam stretch the shorter end or even up the longer one while holding the fabric together.

Even width: the amount of additional width that has to be made even.

Fabric reverse: the side of the fabric on the inside of the garment. All of the marks for the pattern sample are placed on the reverse.

Facing: fabric used to finish garment edges. Facings are cut following the same grain direction as the fabric, using fabric or adhesive knit interfacing. The latter sticks to the fabric with the heat of the iron, never with steam.

Fastener: a small loop of cord, material, metal, etc. that is most commonly used to close a garment by passing a drawstring or button through it.

Fold: indicates that the pattern should be placed on the edge of the folded fabric for cutting.

Foldline or Fabric fold: the line where the fabric is folded to bring the edges together. Often the folded fabric matches the thread direction. Symmetrical pattern pieces are usually cut "on the fold" resulting in complete pieces that are totally equal.

Front: a pattern that matches the front part of a garment.

Fullness: amplitude or extension of a garment in areas where it does not fit tightly to the body.

Gather: to tuck the excess volume on a piece of fabric into many small folds. In long seams, divide the fabric into sections to distribute the width evenly.

Grain (on a pattern): the grain matches the orientation (or the warp) of the fabric and indicates the direction to place the fabric when cutting.

Hem: the piece of fabric that is folded and sewn at the bottom of a garment to give it a proper finish. Therefore, leave a larger margin of fabric for the seams when cutting the pattern.

Hemline: the bottom edge of an item of clothing.

Hip depth (HD): the difference between the hip and waist contours.

Hook and eye: a metal clasp made from two pieces, one is in the shape of a loop while the other is a hook that fits into the first. It is used to fasten together two parts of a garment.

Interfacing: fabric that is placed between the garment fabric and the lining in order to give substance to parts of the garment that need it, such as pocket flaps, buttonholes, the neck, etc. There are sew or iron-on types of interfacing that are made from fabric, knit or wool.

Invisible zipper: a zipper that looks like a seam when it is closed. This type of zipper helps give the garment a cleaner look since it is not noticeable to the eye. To sew invisible zippers, use a special foot that fits your sewing machine and is purchased in the same stores that sell zippers.

Iridescent fabric: fabric made from threads of different colors that give a shimmering appearance.

Knife pleats: permanent pleats that are usually set in the fabric with heat. The fabric needed is three times the measurement of the final garment. As a result, depending on the width of the chosen fabric, up to three panels might have to be joined together to reach the required width.

Lining: a reinforcement on the inside of garments that is used mainly for a clean finish and a graceful reverse. The pattern shows which pieces are the garment's lining. In the case of dresses, linings are often the same size as the pieces whereas coat linings are much bigger.

Loop: a fastening, water knot or similar element that decorates or attaches two ends of a garment.

Mannequin: framework in the shape of the human body, used to assemble, test, alter and display garments.

Mock-up or *toile*: the first sample of a garment, usually made in a white or bone colored fabric. If the garment is symmetrical, only one half is made.

Neckline: the opening on an item of clothing for the neck and part of the chest or back. It is the part of the bust left uncovered by an item of clothing.

Notch: a nick on the edge of a pattern that is used as a guide or point of reference for correct assembly later.

Opening: a cut in the garment for ease of movement or esthetic reasons.

Overlap: pockets or accessories that are placed on the garment.

Pin: a metal nail with a point at one end and a head at the other that is used mainly to fasten fabrics.

Pleat: a fold in the fabric that tightens the garment like a dart, or introduces volume like a tuck. Pleats also have a decorative function. The content of the pleat is the amount of fabric folded in that is not visible from the outside; pleat depth is half of this amount and pleat distance is the distance between two pleats.

Pleating: effect of knife pleats.

Raglan sleeve: a sleeve arrangement with the shoulder in one piece, where the sleeve seam extends from the armhole to the base of the neck and across the center front to the shoulder seam.

Reinforcement: the part of the pattern that is placed on the body to give the garment firmness. Usually, the fabric is doubled or it is reinforced with interfacing.

Ribbon: a narrow strip of fabric mainly used to tie and bind as well as to finish or decorate suits and hats.

Right side of the fabric: the finer side of the fabric, often the side seen in the samples. When sewing, it is on the inside and when the garment is finished it is turned to the outside.

Ruffle: a piece of fabric that is gathered to create fullness at the bottom of hems, cuffs, collars etc. Usually a rectangle but circles or spirals are also used.

Seam: the series of stitches that join two pieces of sewn fabric.

Side: each of the two lateral sides of the human body.

Sleeve: part of the dress or shirt that covers the arm.

Sleeve crown: the upper rounded seam that covers the shoulder joint.

Sleeve Insertion Marks (SIM): marks on the sleeve and torso pattern pieces that determine the exact position to attach the sleeve to the bodice. There are front, back and upper insertion marks; the latter is located at the highest point of the sleeve where it joins the shoulder.

Sleeve with one seam: compared to the two-seamed sleeve, it has less shape and has to be fashioned with pleats or a dart from the elbow to the wrist.

Soak: to shrink or tighten the fabric.

Square: to draw a line at a right angle to a line that already exists.

Strap: an accessory for holding a garment on the body. Straps can be integrated with the garment or they can be external items.

Tassel: a group of threads or cords attached at one end and loose at the other. A tassel dangles as hanging decoration in the shape of a ball or half ball.

Thin: to eliminate excess fabric so that the garment is smoother and lighter.

Thread direction: in fabric, this indicates the direction of the threads in the cloth that are parallel to the edge. Always keep in mind when cutting that the correct thread direction in most garments is vertical to the body.

Toile: see Mock-up.

Transverse lines: orienting symbols marked on the pattern, that join together when the pieces are sewn.

Two-seamed sleeve: a sleeve variation developed from the sleeve with one seam. It has a front seam and a seam at the elbow, which fits the shape of the arm better.

Upper margin or lower margin: the amount of additional cloth needed for a buttoned garment so that the pieces overlap. The upper part of the pattern where the buttonholes are cut is called the "upper margin" and the part underneath where the buttons are sewn is called the "lower margin."

Verticality: the perpendicular nature of a garment with a smooth drape from its own weight.

Vlieseline: a very fine interfacing that is used to reinforce delicate fabrics like silk with the help of an iron.

Waistband: a strap or ribbon with a buckle or clasp for fastening certain types of clothing at the waist.

Waist dart: this dart is made over the curve of the garment's waist.

Zipper: a piece of metal or plastic filled with teeth that interlock or not, depending on the direction the slide is moved. Zippers give a garment a tighter fit.

GLOSSARY OF FABRICS

Acetate: a smooth synthetic fiber with drape that is made from cellulose and can be mixed with cotton or silk.

Bamboo: usually woven with cotton. Bamboo's vertical jointed or pleated nature gives it some elasticity.

Chambray: a tightly woven fabric, made with fine thin thread or cotton.

Crepe: a fabric with a grainy wrinkled surface and a bit of stretch, also called "crep" or "crêpe."

Georgette: a sheer lightweight fabric, somewhat wrinkled, made from silk or synthetics. This fabric is named after the 20th century Parisian designer Madame Georgette de la Plante.

Knit: woven cotton, wool, silk or synthetic fiber that is machine made or handmade, with needles or crochet hook, and is known for its flexibility, elasticity and ability to fit the body.

Lace: decorative semitransparent fabric made by hand and adorned with embroidery.

Organza: a crisp, sheer silk or cotton fabric that can be twisted and shaped like paper.

Ottoman: a corded fabric, often made from silk that is used in dressmaking as well as furniture upholstering.

Paillettes **fabric:** sequined fabric.

Rayon: a smooth, cool lightweight fabric made from wood or cotton fibers, also known as viscose.

Rustic silk: a grainy matte fabric that is thicker than common silk, with a rustic unrefined appearance, also called *bourette.*

Satin: silk or cotton fabric, characterized by its shine and softness.

Sinamay: a fabric made from abaca fiber or sisal, and similar to raffia.

Taffeta: a very bulky silk fabric without a right side or reverse that is iridescent at times.

Tulle: a sheer, lightweight fine mesh fabric made from silk, cotton or synthetics.

Velvet: a plush short pile fabric made from silk, cotton or acetate that is made with two warps and one weft. It should be cut with the nap pointing up for more intense color but usually it is cut in the opposite way and the colors are not very rich once the garment is finished. When working with velvet, never iron heavily since this will crush the pile and change the color – suspend the iron over the velvet instead.

Viscose: see Rayon.

Wool voile: very finely spun, lightweight lamb fur. These characteristics make it an ideal alternative summer fabric.

MEASUREMENT CHART

Name:		Prepared by:		Date:

Observations on the figure:

Posture:

Standard Size	Measured Size	1/2	1/4	1/8
H (Height)				
CC (Chest Circumference)				
WC (Waist Circumference)				
HC (Hip Circumference)				
Individual Hip Depth (the distance between the two extreme points for the HC and WC)				

Standard Values	Measured	Offset	Addition	Assembled
½ Neck Circumference (NC)				
C (Collar)				
BA (Back Arc)				
BL (Back Length)				
HD (Hip Depth)				
CD (Chest Depth)				
FL (Front Length)				
BW (Back Width)				
AD (Armhole Diameter)				
CW (Chest Width)				
½ CC (Chest Circumference)				

Sleeve Measurements	Measured	Formula/Addition	Assembled
SW (Shoulder Width)			
SL (Sleeve Length)			
SCH (Sleeve Crown Height)		BA % 5 to 6 cm	
SlW (Sleeve Width)		AD + addition + 4.5 to 5.5 cm	
UAM (Upper Arm Measurement)		+ addition 3 to 5 cm	
EM (Elbow Measurement)			
WM (Wrist Measurement)			
SEW (Sleeve Edge Width)			

STANDARD MEASUREMENTS (EUROPEAN SIZING)

	NAME OF THE MEASUREMENT	MEASUREMENTS IN CM						
SI	Size	36	38	40	42	44	46	48
H	Height	168	168	168	168	168	168	168
CC	Chest Circumference	80	80	88	92	96	96	104
WC	Waist Circumference	64	68	72	76	80	84	88
HC	Hip Circumference	91	94	97	100	103	106	109
NC	Neck Circumference	34.8	35.4	36	36.6	37.2	37.8	38.4
C	Collar	6.5	6.6	6.7	6.8	6.9	7	7.1
BA	Back Arc	19.3	19.7	20.1	20.5	20.9	21.3	21.7
BL	Back Length	41.2	41.4	41.6	41.8	42	42.2	42.4
HD	Hip Depth	61.4	61.8	62.2	62.6	63	63.4	63.8
CD	Chest Depth	26.5	27.3	28.1	28.9	29.7	30.5	31.3
FL	Front Length	44.1	44.7	45.3	45.9	46.5	47.1	47.7
BW	Back Width	15.5	16	16.5	17	17.5	18	18.5
AD	Armhole Diameter	7.9	8.6	9.3	10	10.7	11.4	12.1
CW	Chest Width	16.6	17.4	18.2	19	19.8	20.6	21.4
SW	Shoulder Width	11.8	12	12.2	12.4	12.6	12.8	13
SL	Sleeve Length	59.3	59.6	59.9	60.2	60.5	60.8	61.1
UAM	Upper Arm Measurement	25.6	26.8	28	29.2	30.4	31.6	32.8
WM	Wrist Measurement	15	15.4	15.8	16.2	16.6	17	17.4
CDA	Chest Dart Angle	11.5°	13°	14.5°	16°	17.5°	19°	20.5°

STANDARD MEASUREMENTS (AMERICAN SIZING)

	NAME OF THE MEASUREMENT	MEASUREMENTS IN INCHES						
SI	Size	4	6	8	10	12	14	16
H	Height	5' 6"	5' 6"	5' 6"	5' 6"	5' 6"	5' 6"	5' 6"
CC	Chest Circumference	31½"	31½"	34⅝"	36¼"	37¹³⁄₁₆"	37¹³⁄₁₆"	40¹⁵⁄₁₆"
WC	Waist Circumference	25³⁄₁₆"	26¾"	28⅜"	29¹⁵⁄₁₆"	31½"	33¹⁄₁₆"	34⅝"
HC	Hip Circumference	35¹³⁄₁₆"	37"	38³⁄₁₆"	39⅜"	40⁹⁄₁₆"	41¾"	42¹⁵⁄₁₆"
NC	Neck Circumference	13¹¹⁄₁₆"	13¹⁵⁄₁₆"	14³⁄₁₆"	14⁷⁄₁₆"	14⅝"	14⅞"	15⅛"
C	Collar	2⁹⁄₁₆"	2⅝"	2⅝"	2¹¹⁄₁₆"	2¾"	2¾"	2¹³⁄₁₆"
BA	Back Arc	7⅝"	7¾"	7¹⁵⁄₁₆"	8¹⁄₁₆"	8¼"	8⅜"	8⁹⁄₁₆"
BL	Back Length	16¼"	16⁵⁄₁₆"	16⅜"	16⁷⁄₁₆"	16⁹⁄₁₆"	16⅝"	16¹¹⁄₁₆"
HD	Hip Depth	24³⁄₁₆"	24⁵⁄₁₆"	24½"	24⅝"	24¹³⁄₁₆"	24¹⁵⁄₁₆"	25⅛"
CD	Chest Depth	10⁷⁄₁₆"	10¾"	11¹⁄₁₆"	11⅜"	11¹¹⁄₁₆"	12"	12⁵⁄₁₆"
FL	Front Length	17⅜"	17⅝"	17¹³⁄₁₆"	18¹⁄₁₆"	18⁵⁄₁₆"	18⁹⁄₁₆"	18¾"
BW	Back Width	6⅛"	6⁵⁄₁₆"	6½"	6¹¹⁄₁₆"	6⅞"	7¹⁄₁₆"	7¼"
AD	Armhole Diameter	3⅛"	3⅜"	3¹¹⁄₁₆"	3¹⁵⁄₁₆"	4³⁄₁₆"	4½"	4¾"
CW	Chest Width	6⁹⁄₁₆"	6⅞"	7³⁄₁₆"	7½"	7¹³⁄₁₆"	8⅛"	8⁷⁄₁₆"
SW	Shoulder Width	4⅝"	4¾"	4¹³⁄₁₆"	4⅞"	4¹⁵⁄₁₆"	5¹⁄₁₆"	5⅛"
SL	Sleeve Length	23⅜"	23⁷⁄₁₆"	23⁹⁄₁₆"	23¹¹⁄₁₆"	23¹³⁄₁₆"	23¹⁵⁄₁₆"	24¹⁄₁₆"
UAM	Upper Arm Measurement	10¹⁄₁₆"	10⁹⁄₁₆"	11"	11½"	12"	12⁷⁄₁₆"	12¹⁵⁄₁₆"
WM	Wrist Measurement	5¹⁵⁄₁₆"	6¹⁄₁₆"	6¼"	6⅜"	6⁹⁄₁₆"	6¹¹⁄₁₆"	6⅞"
CDA	Chest Dart Angle	11.5º	13º	14.5º	16º	17.5º	19º	20.5º